"HEY"
I Choose to Be Successful

Eureka Butler Copyright © 2013 Eureka Butler

All rights reserved.

ISBN-10:1493616579

ISBN-13: 978-1493616572

Jeremiah 29:11 (NIV) "For I know the plans I have for you, " declares the Lord, "plans to prosper you and not to harm you, plans to give you hope and a future."

DEDICATIONS

This Book is dedicated to my family:

To my husband, Manuel Butler, the man whom God has restored back into my life for His purpose. WE have had many trials and challenges. But, God saw fit to bring us out again as "ONE".

To my children, D'Veon, DeJyreka, DeNaysia , whom God has assigned to me as your mother and your caregiver for His purpose. The trials and tribulations came to make us strong.

To my father, Jerome Andrews, the man who showed me how to Work hard for what I want!

To my grandmother, Mattie Ford, who did not say much; although prayed much for me as I was being molded into Gods' servant for his kingdom.

Lastly, to my sisters, sister-in-laws, brother-in-laws, uncles, aunts, cousins, nephews nieces, and friends that may not have understood my purpose, but still loved me in spite of everything.

ACKNOWLEDGMENTS

1 Corinthians 3:6 (NIV) "I planted the seed, Apollos watered it, but God has been making it grow."

I want to give thanks to Bishop Reginald Washington, Sr. and Lady Teresa Washington at Agape Fellowship Center, Quincy, Florida for teaching me how to FAST and how to be business minded. Pastor Stanley Dixon and Prophetess Patsy Dixon at Anointed Word Christian Center for teaching me how to PRAY, how to be a Servant, and how to Love my husband. Pastor Jesse Nightingale and Lady Terri Nightingale at Guiding Light Ministries for showing me how to Walk in my Calling from God, as a Servant.

To the best Protector I know. I thank God for not turning His back on me as He promised in His Word, "He will never leave me nor forsake me." (Hebrews 13:5, Deuteronomy 31:8, Deuteronomy 31:6, Hebrews 13:6, 1 Peter 5:7, Hebrews 13:5-6, Matthew 28:20; Joshua 1:5)

Table of Contents

Dedication	2
Acknowledgements	3
Foreword	6
Chapter One: What is Success?	11
Chapter Two: The Heart	14
Exercise 1: Attitude	26
Exercise 2: 5 Ways to Deal with Guilt	28
Exercise 3: A Heart for Success	35
Exercise 4: Corruption and Greed List	49
Chapter Three: The Soul	67
Recognition of Sin	70
Elimination of Sin	71
Eliminate Routine of Sin	72
Exercise 5: "Longing fulfilled"	78
Exercise 6: The Soul Search for Success	79

Chapter Four: The Mind	82
Exercise 7: Success Mindset	86
Exercise 8: Set yourself free of the little gods	95
Exercise 9: Tearing Down Strongholds	108
Chapter Five: Division in the Church	110
Chapter Six: Pressing Toward the Goal	118
Chapter Seven: The Strength of Success	122
Chapter Eight: Fasting and Prayer	132
Neglecting God and others by……..	142
The by-products of living for God……	143
The Story of Job and Wealth	144
" A Recipe for Success"	147

FOREWORD

"SUCCESS" through loving God with all my heart, soul, mind and strength...

"Faith is the substance of things hoped for, the evidence of things not seen." Hebrews 11:1 KJV

Everyday is a day to be successful. The words, **"I Choose To Be Successful"** can open our heart, mind and soul to receive the divine wisdom of God. If we want to be successful in our marriage, as parents, on our jobs, as an entrepreneur, and in life, we can no longer be hesitated about speaking out in **" Faith"**.

There are four simple words that you can speak with "faith" that will open your heart, soul, and mind to receive the divine wisdom of God. I need for you to take a deep breathe and take your mind off everything. I need for you to speak these words with "faith" in your heart, soul and mind; **"Let there be light!"** Speaking these words over every complicated and mystified situations will stir up the fire in your heart, soul and mind. The power of God will transfer like ever before in every situation in your life.

In James 1:17, (NKJV) "Every good gift and every perfect gift is from above, and comes down from the Father of lights, with whom there is no variation or shadow of turning". The power of God is in the Word of God. In James 1:17, God wants all of us to have what is good and perfect gifts. We not only have good health. Today, we have the perfect gift of health. We have gone beyond a good marriage. Today, we have the perfect gift of marriage, as well as, we have the perfect gift of parenting. We don't have to settle for a good job. Today, we have a perfect gift of a job. For all the entrepreneurs and business owners, we have the perfect gift of entrepreneurship. Today, we have the perfect gift of ideas for success.

Right at this moment, in your "Faithful" filled voice, Shout! "Let there be light!" Repeat these four simple words in every situation and **believe**. Here are some of my favorite "faith" speaking words:

I speak: *"**Let there be light in my marriage!**"*

*"**Let there be Light in my finances!**"*

*"**Let there be light concerning this mortgage payment, light bill and car payment!**"*

You are capable of speaking "Light" to all of life matters. When you have finished speaking the "Light", you should feel a release of heaviness. You have released the heaviness of the burdensome that were associated with worrying and doubting. "Let there be Light"........At this present moment, everything that you have spoken in "faith" right before your eyes have been illuminated.

INTRODUCTION

To simply know that you have the power within you to be alive, do and create anything in your life is giving yourself permission to be the brilliant, radiant, magnificent, and divine individual you were chosen to be. There are countless secrets to success that have been revealed to me as I began my journey back with God. My top three are:

1st Secret To Know "Whose you are...?"

I John 4:4 (KJV) "Ye are of God, little children, and have overcome them: because greater is he that is in you, than he that is in the world."

It is easy to be frightened by the wickedness we see all around us and overwhelmed by the problems we face. Evil is obviously much stronger than we are. John assures us, however, that God is even stronger. He will conquer all evil and that his Spirit and his Word lives in our hearts!

2nd Secret is a "Vision..."

Proverbs 29:18 (KJV) "Where there is no vision, the people perish: but he that keepeth the law, happy is he."

Where there is ignorance or rejection of God; crime and sin run wild. Public morality depends on the knowledge of God's law. In order for both nations and individuals to function well, people must know God's ways and keep his rules. Having God's Word means little, if we are not obeying them.

3rd Secret is "Faith..."

James 2:26 (KJV) "For as the body without the spirit is dead, so faith without works is dead also."

We have to be in motion. "ACTION" needs to present in our lives. In James 2:25, when Israel's spies came to the city, Rahab hid them and helped them escape. In this way she demonstrated faith in God's purpose for Israel.

We have Greatness, We have a Vision, and We have Faith to overcome. With these three (3) Secrets; we can cast down fear, we are no longer frightened, nor intimidated of the things of this evil world. Now, its time to march forward in our destiny as successful God-fearing kingdom minded individuals.

CHAPTER ONE

WHAT IS SUCCESS?

What is success? For some, success means owning a big house, driving a fancy car and going on exotic vacations. For several, success may look like having inner peace, an abundance of love and happiness, and living a life of integrity. Then there is success in your marriage, as a parent, on your job or as a business owner. For others, success can be a combination of both! In any case, success is whatever you make it signify. Here are six steps to being successful.

1. Deepen your spiritual relationship. Success begins with you. Strengthening your relationship with God is the most indispensable step to knowing who/whose you are at the foundation of life. When you know who/whose you are, you can be who you are. And when you can be who you are, without fear, then anything and everything is promising.

2. Take full ownership of who you are. Taking ownership means not creating excuses; not blaming others, and not using your past or circumstances as reasons why you are not capable of being successful. When you know who/whose you are and can still love all of you, both your light and past darkness; you can own who you are. Taking ownership and being responsible for what you think, what you say and what you do is vital to truly being successful. Remember success **starts and begins** with you.

3. Understanding that your purpose is who/whose you are, not what you do. People often ask me, "How do I find my purpose?" Your purpose is not hiding under a rock. You don't need to search for it because it has always been with you. You were born with a precise purpose the day you were created. I have found that I am the most active when I am helping others deepen their awareness about themselves. If you are on the quest to "finding" your purpose, think of your most recent memory where you felt the most active and happy. What were you doing? Who were you being? Begin with the understanding that your purpose is a state of being.

4. Commit to realizing, redefining and realigning your vision. Your vision can be as big or small as you want it to be. The important thing here is to align your vision with purpose. Once you uncover your purpose and who you are as a human being in the world, the next step would be to ask yourself; "Well, if this is who I am in the world, then what would I be doing? Your vision is the reason "why" you wake up every morning. It's your "big motivation." What's the legacy that you want to leave behind?

5. Being a conscious creator. To be a conscious creator of your world means you need to be taking committed action. It means that you are awake in your life, aware of your purpose and your vision. You are willing to do whatever it takes to have the life that you want. **"ACTION"** is the avenue to success. If you are feeling stuck in an area of your life, **"GET MOVING"** and take **ACTION**. If you are not happy with a situation in your life, then **"DO SOMETHING"** about it.

6. Be responsible for the energy in your space. Everything is energy. God, money, love, fear, the universe, your thoughts, words, and actions; all are energy in your space. Everyday you need to take responsibility for the energy you convey into this space. This simple piece of wisdom can be life altering, if you apply it to, not only to the energy that you are allowing in, but also to the energy that you are putting into your heart, soul and mind. Be aware of how the energy is showing up in your life. What kind of thoughts do you have when you wake up? When something goes unexpected, do you usually blame yourself or someone else? Remember that your thoughts, words, and actions; when aligned, will produce unimaginable success in your life.

CHAPTER TWO

THE HEART

The Heart is mentioned over 900 times in the bible. Therefore, Success begins in the heart. **"Command your success in your Heart."**

When I endeavored upon my first business journey, from the bottom of my heart, I wanted to make a difference in the world. There was no job description that allowed me to do just what I wanted to do for the world, or the freedom that being self-employed gives you, or the income potential. So, by God's grace and help, I established the business that would make a difference and to help change lives of individuals in the world. The business was working with individuals with developmental disabilities; physical and mental.

I designed the business with a heart for serving people. The success of managing a business became a challenge for me and my family. Operating a business turned out to be more involved, than I might possibly imagine it would have entailed. My vision easily got off course in the overwhelming whirl of details and the pressure of bringing in money for the family. It is no surprise one can end up dispirited and burnt-out; losing confidence, passion and direction, because I was that one person that did all of those things. God was in my life, but not the center of my business. My marriage was not healthy. Nevertheless, my kids and family valued receiving what they wanted, whenever they desired something. Therefore, I became burned out from the pressure of succeeding; complaining about all the long hours and paperwork.

I really lost the passion and direction to why I wanted the business in the beginning. The business was to help individuals; not for me to focus on making money. I lost the concept of helping; and got too much involved in loving the wealth and luxury from the business revenues.

My family and I had the nice home, nice cars, nice vacations, and luxury spending. But, as the business owner, I was missing something. That something was loving God with all my heart, soul, mind, and strength. By me not focusing on the things of God; the love of money became the core of my business. Because I was buying and spending like I wanted ; and my family, as well. My marriage was not priority. Money became precedence and the god of life. *1 Timothy 6:10 (NIV) "For the love of money is a root of all kinds of evil. Some people, eager for money, have wandered from the faith and pierced themselves with many griefs."*

Through the love of money and ungodly choices that were made, God allowed some things to happen in my life. I divorced my husband. Immediately afterwards, the business was closed by the state agency. I became devastated. After trying to hold things together and to build another business, I lost faith in myself and God. Without faith in God, I became misplaced in this evil world.

My father and family members lives in Jacksonville, Florida. Therefore, I moved to Jacksonville, Florida to get my life back on course with God. Also, the moved to Jacksonville, Florida was an escape from all the pessimism of my home town. During my season in Jacksonville, Florida, <u>*"I"*</u> was able to find God all over again; because he never left me, I left Him. My husband and I remarried. Currently, we are working together on future projects.

Although, we still have our challenges, God is the core of our marriage and family. I can speak with my "faith" filled voice, "I am loving God with all my heart, soul, mind, and with His strength.

Deuteronomy 6:5 (NIV) "Love the Lord your God with all your heart and with all your soul and with all your strength."

The First and Greatest commandment Jesus said" was loving God with all of our self," is the first and greatest commandment (Matthew 22:37-39). This command, combined with the command to love your neighbor (Leviticus 19:18), encompasses all the other Old Testament laws.

2 Chronicles 12:14 (KJV) "And he did evil, because he prepared not his heart to seek the Lord."

Rehoboam, son of Solomon, son of David, and son of Jesse. Rehoboam's story is tragic because he "had set his heart on seeking the Lord." How tragic a description of the grandson of David, who had been called "a man after God's own heart" (1Samuel 13:14) failed. It is dangerous to put off responding to God. God asks us to firm commitment; and unless we respond by not trusting him completely, we will find ourselves alienated from him.

In 2 Chronicles 12:1-14, "Israel" refers to Judah, the southern kingdom. During the first three years on the throne, Rehoboam attempted to obey God, and as a result Judah prospered. Then, at his peak of popularity and power, he abandoned God. The result was destruction because God allowed Judah to be conquered by Egypt. How could this happen?

Often it is more difficult to be a believer in good times than in bad times. Tough times push us toward God; but easy times can make us feel self-sufficient and self-satisfied. When everything is going right, guard your faith closely. In 2 Chronicles 12:6-8, God eased his judgment when Israel's leaders confessed their sins, humbled themselves, and recognized God's justice in punishing them. It is never too late to repent, even in the midst of punishment.

Regardless of what we have done, God is willing to receive us back into his arms. Are you alone and struggling, because sin has broken your relationship with God? Confession and humility will open the door to receiving God's mercy.

Psalm 112:7 (KJV) "He shall not be afraid of evil tidings; his heart is fixed, trusting in the Lord."

"**No Fear**" of bad news.... my heart is steadfast and completing trusting in the Lord my God with all my heart, soul, mind, and strength . One particular afternoon, I drifted into a deep sleep. In my sleep, I was contemplating on being with an ex. As soon as adultery (sex) was getting ready to make a move, the dog woke me up with a bark. Then, there was a knock at the door. As I approached the door, a police officer was standing looking in the glass of the door.

"I am done with fear this day" came out of my mouth quickly. I immediately opened the door. As the door was opening, fear immediately exited out the front door. Then I said to the police officer, "Yes, may I help you?", with a smile". The officer said, "Is James ----- here?" I said no James--- then, he said "are you sure?" I said, "yes". He said "well this is the last known address for him on file".

I said, "I'm sorry sir". Then he apologized for the mishap and walked away. Immediately, four police officers came from both sides of the house. I was like "WOW!".

At that moment in my life, my marriage was going through some trials and tribulations. Therefore, I was not so ecstatic with my life, I was just holding on to the Word of God. I was believing and trusting that God had everything under control. You see that old ex was that adultery spirit trying to creep back in my mind. The devil tried to get a hold of me in my sleep, but God intervened.

Before I could open the front door to see what the police wanted, the devil immediately tried to influence fear at the front door. At that current time in my life, I was late on the Mercedes payment, I was dealing with a disgruntled tenant, and some legal issues were still present. The devil wanted me to speak and think negatively; but I shut the devil down quickly!

Success is a process. Your past or current circumstances may bring fear, but, you have to cast down that negativity…. quickly. In 2 Corinthians 10:5 (KJV) states, *"Casting down imaginations, and every high thing that exalteth itself against the knowledge of God, and bringing into captivity every thought to the obedience of Christ;"* God has given us the power to cast down every evil imagination and thoughts to Christ. Give those evil imaginations and thoughts to Christ. Christ knows better what to do with them than we do. There are no assessments involved, just cast down! **Spirit-empowered believers** must capture every thought and yield it to Christ.

I am so much in synch and in love with God that fear of the natural is not an option for me anymore. I speak and believe everyday, **"Let there be light to my success!"** God has every part and every aspect of my life in prospective. Fear of the past no longer drives my future! If God can change my heart, mind and soul; He can do the same for you. **Just believe and have that unshakable faith.**

Psalm 112:8 (NIV) "His heart is secure, he will have no fear; in the end he will look in triumph on his foes."

Too many times in my marriage, the words, "we do not have a future together" were spoken. Words are powerful and the tongue is dangerous. Proverbs 18:21 (KJV) *"Death and life are in the power of the tongue, and those who love it will eat its fruit."*

When disagreements came during the season of healing from the divorce, I quickly said, "we do have a future together." I kept repeating those words into the atmosphere, until I know longer have to say them anymore. Now, we both know that "we do have a future together'"; and the devil no longer controls our actions or thoughts. Those negative words were just confirming that healing was taking place and the devil was mad. When the negative transformed into positive, those positive words allowed God to guide our marriage. I have found out during my season of healing from the divorce; that it was easy to sign those divorce papers than to work on the marriage. God has taught me through the Word, how to stand on HIS promises concerning marriage; not man's marriage, with peace. Now, I can speak "We are going to be the Man and Woman God called us to be as "ONE."

Afterwards, I can speak "Let there be light in my marriage."

I truly believe what His Word says about death and life are in the power of the tongue. Once I started speaking life into my marriage, God began to move in the healing process. Once I was healed, then I was able to receive God's power to cast every evil imagination and thought concerning my marriage.

Then, I started believing on these scriptures for the "Light of love"

Genesis 1:27-28 (NIV) " *27 So God created mankind in his own image, in the image of God he created them; male and female he created them. 28 God blessed them and said to them, "Be fruitful and increase in number; fill the earth and subdue it. Rule over the fish in the sea and the birds in the sky and over every living creature that moves on the ground."*

Genesis 2:21-24 (NIV) "*21 So the Lord God caused the man to fall into a deep sleep; and while he was sleeping, he took one of the man's ribs and closed up the place with flesh. 22 Then the Lord God made a woman from the rib he had taken out of the man, and he brought her to the man. 23 "This is how bone of my bones and flesh of my flesh; she shall be called "woman" for she was taken out of man," 24 For this reason a man will leave his father and mother and be united to his wife, and they will become one flesh."*

1 Corinthians 13:4-8 (NIV) *"4 Love is patient, love is kind. It does not envy, it does not boast, it is not proud. 5 It is not rude, it is not self-seeking, it is not easily angered, it keeps no record of wrongs. Love does not delight in evil but rejoices with the truth. 7 It always protects, always trust, always hopes, always perseveres."*

Colossians 3:14 (NIV) *"And over all these virtues put on love, which binds them all together in perfect unity."*

Then the "Light of Marriage"

1 Corinthians 7:2 (ESV) *"But because of temptations to sexual immorality, each man should have his own wife and each woman her own husband."*

Malachi 2:14 (ESV) *"But you say, "Why does he not?" Because the LORD was witness between you and the wife of your youth, to whom you have been faithless, though she is your companion and your wife by covenant."*

Ecclesiastes 4:9-12 (NASB)*"Two are better than one because they have a good return for their labor. 10 For, if either of them falls, the one will lift up his companion. But woe to the one who falls when there is not another to lift him up. 11 Furthermore, if two lie down together they keep warm, but how can one be warm alone? 12 And if one can overpower him who is alone, two can resist him. A cord of three strands is not quickly torn apart."* **(The cord of three strands: God, husband, and wife)**

Ephesians 5:25-29 (NASB) "25 *Husbands, love your wives, just as Christ also loved the church and gave Himself up for her, 26 so that He might sanctify her, having cleansed her by the washing of water with the word, 27 that He might present to Himself the church in all her glory, having no spot or wrinkle or any such thing; but that she should be holy and blameless. 28 So husbands ought also to love their own wives as their own bodies. He who loves his own wife loves himself; 29 for no one ever hated his own flesh, but nourishes and cherishes it, just as Christ also does the church,"*

1 Peter 3:1-6 (NASB) "*1 In the same way, you wives, be submissive to your own husbands so that even if any of them are disobedient to the word, they may be won without a word by the behavior of their wives, 2 as they observe your chaste and respectful behavior. 3 Your adornment must not be merely external—braiding the hair, and wearing gold jewelry, or putting on dresses; 4 but let it be the hidden person of the heart, with the imperishable quality of a gentle and quiet spirit, which is precious in the sight of God. 5 For in this way in former times the holy women also, who hoped in God, used to adorn themselves, being submissive to their own husbands; 6 just as Sarah obeyed Abraham, calling him lord, and you have become her children if you do what is right without being frightened by any fear."*

Proverbs 4: 20-22 (NIV) "*20 My son, pay attention to what I say; turn your ear to my words. 21 Do not let them out of your sight, keep them within your heart; 22 for they are life to those who find them and health to one's whole body."*

Your heart holds your success. It is God's Word that bestows success upon your life. Not man's words; but God's Word. Prohibit people from speaking negatively into your ears. Man cannot catch a glimpse of your future or your success. When people start talking negative or saying things that is not in alignment with your success; stop them immediately, cover your ears or just walk away. Always remember that God knows the extent of your success and the journey for you to get there; not man. Verse 22 states that God's Word is life and health to your whole body. Therefore, this day and everyday forward, speak ,"Let there be light to my success, to my life, to my health, in my marriage, job and businesses,..........."

Proverbs 15:13-14 (NIV) *"13 A happy heart makes the face cheerful, but heartache crushes the spirit. 14 The discerning heart seeks knowledge, but the mouth of a fool feeds on folly."*

In this present day, this smile on my face is not because of homes, cars or money. This smile originated from the Lord, our God, in my heart that makes me joyful. I know longer strive for happiness. I strive for "JOY." Psalm 35:9 (KJV) *" And my soul shall be joyful in the Lord; it shall rejoice in his salvation."* All the money-oriented and lavishness things are only temporary and they make people happy. When it disappears, what do you have? Nothing! Then, you are left with a broken heart that has no value. But, the heart of God is eternal. The heart of God holds your success. The heart of God brings "JOY". Begin to welcome God in your heart. Allow God to dwell in your heart on a daily basis; not only when you want something. Now speak these word, **"I thank God for a JOYFUL heart."**

We can allow God in our hearts. But, not hearts that dwell in dirt, filth and mess. You must be discerning of what goes in your heart. Discerning is having or showing good judgment towards something. Therefore, be discerning of what you read, the music you listen to, the shows you watch on TV, and the people you talk to. Your surroundings are what influence your heart and mind. Our heart and mind has to be as healthy as our bodies. **Watch was goes into your heart!**

Proverbs 15:15(NIV) *"All the days are of the oppressed are wretched, but the cheerful heart has a continual feast."*

Attitude is a component of success. We cannot always control what happens to us, but we can control our attitude towards the situation. We will get the so-called "no", "are you sure?", "you don't have the education or training," as one is preparing to be successful. It is our attitude that will twist that little "no" into a Big "YES". The secret to success is having a cheerful heart with a perfect attitude. A perfect attitude focuses on things that are **true, pure, and lovely**.

NOTES:

_____
_____
_____
_____
_____
_____

Exercise 1: ATTITUDE

Fill in the blanks: (Use the alphabet to fill in the numbers and add the numbers together. The final number will give you the percentage of your ATTITUDE when moving forward, for example A=1, B=2, C=3, D=4, E=5,.. I= 9......, T=20....U=21.....)

A_____

T_____

T_____

I_____

T_____

U_____

D_____

E_____

ATTITUDE =_____%

Speak "Let there be light in my attitude". This day forward, I will have _____% attitude towards my success.

Philippians 4:7 (NIV) "And the peace of God, which transcends all understanding, will guard your hearts and minds in Christ Jesus. "

What is guilt? Guilt is a cognitive or an emotional experience that occurs when a person realizes or believes accurately or not that he or she has compromised his or her own standards of conduct or has violated a moral standard, and bears significant responsibility for that violation. Guilt is the remorseful awareness of having done something wrong. Our past sins bring about anxiety, doubt and worrying; which leads to guilt. The prophetess that I served under told me that I was dealing with more of personal guilt than the negativity of the people in the world. Therefore, I continuously had to speak death to guilt, fear, anxiety, doubt, and worrying of my past sins. I can remember, I felt bad about how I treated God and my family. My own guilty conscience was holding me back from future success; than people. It is very important not to blame others for not being successful. Success comes from "ACTION" of self; not people. WE have to find the "peace" of God in our hearts from the past sin/wrongdoings; instead of feeling guilty about something you cannot change. The "true peace" comes from knowing that your success is in God.

Guilty people punish themselves if they have no opportunity to compensate the transgression that caused them to feel guilty.

Exercise 2: 5 Ways to Deal with Guilt

1. Recognize the kind of guilt you have and its purpose.

(For example: If you feel guilty about eating five chocolate bars in a row or for focusing on a career with an 80-hour work week over spending time with your family.)

A. List a "guilt", in your life at this present moment:

_____
_____
_____
_____

2. Make amends or changes sooner rather than later.

(If a spouse has cheated, make amends with the other spouse today; not next week or if your words offended someone, ask them to forgive you today; not tomorrow or next week.)

B. The Amend or Change:

_____
_____
_____
_____

3. Accept you did something wrong, but move on.

If you did something wrong or hurtful, you will have to accept that you cannot change the past. But, you can make amends for your behavior, if and when it's appropriate. Do apologize, make up for the inappropriate behavior in a timely manner, then "let it go." The more you believe you need to do something more, the more it will continue to bother you and interfere with your relationship with others.

C. How did you move on?

_____
_____
_____

4. Learning from our behaviors.

Guilt's purpose is not to make us feel bad just for the sake of it. The feeling of guilt is trying to get your attention so that you can learn something from the experience. If we learn from our behavior, we will be less likely to do it again in the future.

D. What did you learn?

_____
_____
_____

5. Perfection does not exist in anyone. *(Proverbs 3:10 (NIV) "As it is written: "There is no one righteous, not even one;")*

Nobody is perfect, not even our friends or family members who appear to lead perfect, guilt free-lives. Striving for perfection in any element of our lives is a recipe for failure; since it is not attainable.

What about feeling guilty about stealing during a certain phase in your younger years that caused you to go to jail? Now, you have this criminal record and you believe you cannot move forward. **" Let there be Light in this criminal record"**. Do not say "**my** criminal record", but "**the** criminal record" because this guilt no longer controls your future. It's present, but the criminal record does not belong to you.

Now, you can follow these same steps in Exercise 2. "<u>Yourself</u>" will be the person that needs to forgive "<u>you</u>." You can't change the past, but you can take action towards the future. List ways to amend or change things. Possibly, some of your changes would be to complete a trade or vocational program, finding an occupation, or business that does not require a background screening, or become self-employed. You have to know and have "faith" that your destiny is already set; and you have victory over your past sins and over all past and wrongful acts. Through the death of Jesus Christ, on the cross, your sins have been forgiven. **Therefore, remove the guilt and let's move forward in "success".**

Proverbs 16:1 (NLT) *"We can make our own plans, but the Lord gives the right answer."*

It is very important to know that not all success is God's success. Your plans have to link up with God's Word. So why make plans when God has the last word? We have to demonstrate some type of **ACTION.** Success is a choice; not mandatory. You have to choose to be successful. Choosing to be successful is aligning your lifestyle and your way of thinking with the Word of God. God wants you to utilize your mind to seek the advice of others; and to plan. If we show God how bad we desire something and live a Jesus Christ- like life; he will step-in to direct the path to success. He will continue to direct you according to His "will" and purpose for your life. Even though we may be seeking advice from others, we still have to seek God to make sure it is his direction; not man's direction. As you plan, remember to always ask God for his guidance; because the final outcome of your success or plan comes from the reply of His tongue.

Matthew 9:3-8 (NIV) "3 At this, some of the teachers of the law said to themselves, "This fellow is blaspheming!" 4 Knowing their thoughts, Jesus said, "Why do you entertain evil thoughts in your hearts? 5 Which is easier: to say, 'Your sins are forgiven,' or to say, 'Get up and walk'? 6 But I want you to know that the Son of Man has authority on earth to forgive sins." So he said to the paralyzed man, "Get up, take your mat and go home." 7 Then the man got up and went home. 8 When the crowd saw this, they were filled with awe; and they praised God, who had given such authority to man."

You know longer need to allow your past to bring evil thoughts into you "Success." Majority of you are allowing your past to keep you from being successful. Unwanted thoughts can make you feel anxious or depressed. Unwanted thoughts keep you from enjoying your life and future success. Some thoughts may be poverty, failure, lack of, anxiety, insults from the past, and dehumanization. **YOU** have to learn how to cast down these thoughts immediately and move forward. *2 Corinthians 10:5 (NIV) "We demolish arguments and every pretension that sets itself up against the knowledge of God, and we take captive every thought to make it obedient to Christ."*

Now pray, **"I decree and declare everything that is misaligned to come into divine alignment and that I may have the heart of Jesus Christ. Therefore, I will seek things above and not beneath. I decree and declare that I wear the helmet of salvation to protect my heart and mind from negative thoughts that would derail God's purpose and plans for me in Jesus name. Amen!"**

Jeremiah 29:11 (NIV) "For I know the plans I have for you," declares the Lord, "plans to prosper you and not to harm you, plans to give you hope and a future.

In this moment, start asking God to help you to look at the world through his eyes of success; rather than the eyes of failure. Ask God for wisdom, as you are being shown the things through his eyes, concerning what he has called you to do/be. In Matthew 9:5, Jesus is showing us that it is easier to say, "Your sins are forgiven", than to reverse paralysis. I am talking about easier for man; because nothing is too hard for Him.

Jesus did heal the man's legs to back up his Word. But, you as Christians, can easily say, "your sins are forgiven". Jesus has given us the power to speak these words. **Believe** and have the **faith** concerning the Word of God. I speak right now in the name of Jesus, **"Your sins have been forgiven."**

Get up right now, whether you are sitting in a chair or on the sofa. Literally, get up and begin walking into your success. Remember the Word "ACTION". Walking is Action! Walk until you feel it in your heart. Walk until you believe you are Successful. Walk until you start speaking your Success in the atmosphere. WALK into your Destiny.

How do you feel? What are your thoughts?

_____
_____
_____
_____
_____
_____
_____
_____
_____
_____
_____
_____
_____
_____
             _____

Matthew 12:33-37(NIV) *33 "Make a tree good and its fruit will be good, or make a tree bad and its fruit will be bad, for a tree is recognized by its fruit. 34 You brood of vipers, how can you who are evil say anything good? For the mouth speaks what the heart is full of. 35 A good man brings good things out of the good stored up in him, and an evil man brings evil things out of the evil stored up in him. 36 But I tell you that everyone will have to give account on the day of judgment for every empty word they have spoken. 37 For by your words you will be acquitted, and by your words you will be condemned."*

    Religious leaders accused Jesus of getting his powers from Beelzebub (Luke 11). Jesus is reminding leaders what comes out of their mouth reveals what's in their hearts. Being successful is being a leader in one's eyesight. You cannot just think about yourself and how successful you have become. God brings his success to his believers, so that non-believers will want the same passion by following God. Always remember, **not all success is God's success.** In this present day, you are seeking God's success. Therefore, you have to be cautious of what comes out of your mouth. Cleaning up your speech in front of an audience is not enough for God. Your heart has to be pure and clean. Your attitude and motives have to be connected with God. You may or can give a great speech, but God judges your heart. A great speech can take you places, but a clean and pure heart can take you around the world with success. I rather have a clean heart than a great speech. Today, you must ask the Holy Spirit to fill your heart, soul and mind with new attitude and new motives; as a result, your speech will be cleansed at His source.

Exercise 3: A Heart for Success Exercise

Below are four key steps that you need to search within your heart that will provide you with the clarity, focus, and direction you need for creating success in all areas of your life!

1. Always begin by IDENTIFYING YOUR VALUES. Values are "what's important" to you, in essence, they are the unconscious "bottom lines" that drive your behavior on a subconscious level. You often get into trouble because we are only vaguely aware of these subconscious bottom lines and they are often contradicted by your conscious behavior. When you clearly identify these bottom lines, you bring them to a conscious level of awareness, which in turn gives you the ability to align your actions and intentions with what's really important to you. When your values are clear, your decisions are easy, and your directions are focused.

List five values that is important to you today; not next week or next year, but today: (For example: purchasing a new home, starting a business, restoring your marriage, losing weight, finding a new job, and so on.)

A._____

B._____

C._____

D._____

2. CLARIFY YOUR GOALS. When it comes to achieving your goals, failure most often happens when you have not clearly defined what it is you truly want. Identify what you want in each area of your life. If you cannot clearly communicate what you want your relationships and finances to look like, the path to getting there will be extremely hard to see. Be as specific as possible. For example, if you want to lose weight, how much do you want to lose and by when? If you want a better job, define "better", what does it look like?

A._____

B._____

C._____

D._____

3. IDENTIFY & DISMANTLE YOUR STOPPERS. What is keeping you "stuck"?.... Procrastination? Fear? A lack of time or money? Brainstorm as many reasons as you can for not achieving your dreams. Once you have identified your specific stoppers, the key is to dismantle them and accept responsibility for moving past them. There are many wonderful examples of people overcoming incredible odds to create the life they want to live and you can too.

A._____

B._____

C._____

D._____

E._____

F._____

G. _____

H. _____

I._____

4. TAKE ACTION.

Finally, take action, today. Without taking action, you will not achieve your goals. Take action every day, no matter how small the steps may seem. Remember, success is never an accident; it's a choice. Take full responsibility for your future today by actively engaging in steps to success. (For example; I will walk for 30 minutes a day to lose weight or I will seek out counselors to help with my marriage, and so forth.)

A._____

B._____

C._____

D._____

E._____

F._____

G._____

H._____

I._____

Now, think on those great tasks to success . Here are ways of knowing that the Holy Spirit is filling your heart with great tasks for success:

Personal endowment

Haggai 2:5 (NIV) *"This is what I covenanted with you when you came out of Egypt. And my Spirit remains among you. Do not fear."*

The Israelites were led from captivity in Egypt to their promised land. They were God's chosen people; guided and cared for by his Holy Spirit. Therefore, YOU are God's chosen people for "success." Since you know that you are God's chosen people, allow Him to guide and care for you by his Holy Spirit. Although God had punished the Israelites for their sins, he kept his promise and never left them. (Exodus 29:45-46 NIV…."45 Then *I will dwell among the Israelites and be their God. 46 They will know that I am the Lord their God, who brought them out of Egypt so that I might dwell among them. I am the Lord their God"*). Your sins have consequences. Proverbs 11:21 (NIV) *"Be sure of this: The wicked will not go unpunished, but those who are righteous will go free."* **No sin goes unpunished**! Accept the punishment and move forward to success. No matter what took place in the past or your strongholds , *you have been forgiven through repentance.*

In your current success, no matter the difficulties you may face or how frustrating the task; God's Holy Spirit is with you, guiding and directing your destiny.

Spirit is Wise   Isaiah 11:2-3 (NIV)

2 The Spirit of the Lord will rest on him-

the Spirit of wisdom and of understanding,

the Spirit of counsel and power,

the Spirit of knowledge and of the fear of the Lord-

3 and he will delight in the fear of the Lord.

He will not judge by what he sees with his eyes,

or decide by what hears with is ears;

Holy

Psalm 51:13 (NIV) *"Restore to me the joy of your salvation and grant me a willing spirit, to sustain me."*

    David had sinned with Bathsheba and had just been confronted by Nathan the prophet. David felt stagnant in life and his faith. David felt he was just going through the motions and seemed far from his destiny. But he cried out to God and was restored. You have to be like David concerning your past sins/wrongdoings. You need to cry out more to God so he can bring restoration in your life. Find yourself a quiet place to have some crying time with God. I have found much success crying in my bedroom closet. When I come out my bedroom closet; my eyes are puffy and I have a running nose.

The closet cry is all worth it; because the heaviness is lifted! When you cry out to God, be sincere! God already knows what you need and how you are feeling. If you are feeling some hurt and pain, cry out and tell God "in Jesus name" that you are hurting. If you really don't know how you are going to make it. Cry out and ask God to show and teach you how to make it each day "in Jesus name."

Matthew 6:34 (NIV) *"Therefore, do not worry about tomorrow, for tomorrow will worry about itself. Each day has enough trouble of its own."*

We have to confess our sins/wrongdoings daily to God. We still may have to face some earthly consequences, as David did. But, God just want your full attention; by confessing and repenting each day to him. Once you can confess and repent, then God can do His work in you. Say, *"Restore to me the joy of your salvation and grant me a willing spirit, to sustain me...* in Jesus Name. Amen" Psalm 51:12 NIV. Believe that you have been restored and speak to your success.

Good

Psalm 143:10 (NIV) *"Teach me to do your will, for you are my God; may your good Spirit lead me on level ground."*

David prayer was for God to teach him His will; not David's own will. Your success is not your success; it's God's success.

Everything about God is good and perfect. By asking God for guidance for structure to your success, awakens your heart to "HIS Will and His Purpose."

Presence of God

Psalm 139:7 (NIV) *"Where can I go from your Spirit? Where can I flee from your presence?"*

God is everywhere. God created heaven and earth and everything in it. Therefore, you need to open your heart to the greater things in life. I am glad to know that God's presence is everywhere. Therefore, I will never go astray from His Holy Spirit, again. No matter how successful you become, you can never be far from God's comforting presence (Romans 8:35-39). Therefore, when those past evils thoughts, strongholds, and sins/wrong actions begin to arise during the process of succeeding; the Holy Spirit can intervene on your behalf to cast them down immediately.

Remember, its not the success that gets you closer to God; **its your heart that gets you closer to God.**

Power

Acts 1:8 (NIV) *"But you will receive power when the Holy Spirit comes on you; and you will be my witnesses in Jerusalem, and in all Judea and Samaria, and to the ends of the earth."*

You need the power of the Holy Spirit for God's success. The "power" that is received from the Holy Spirit is courage, boldness, confidence, insight, ability, and authority. You need all these gifts to fulfill God's mission for success. God knows all of our hearts. But you have to allow God in your heart; so He can show you He is trustworthy.

I had to change my environment and location. Therefore, God allowed me to come to Jacksonville, Florida to cleanse my heart and renew His Holy Spirit within me. At first, I thought I was running from people because of the shame and guilt that had built up on the inside of me. Really, I was running to my restoration place; for the healing and deliverance that needed to take place on the inside of me. Now, I am walking and speaking in the prophetic to many of God's people. God allowed my running away, I thought was for bad, for something good and perfect. Genesis 50:20 (NIV) *"You intended to harm me, but God intended it for good to accomplish what is now being done, the saving of many lives."*

Now, I have a heart of God that is "teachable" for His success. I did some things that God did not approve. I was disobedient in my marriage, to my children, to my family, to the church, and business. Because of the disobedience, God allowed me to go through some trials to win him back.

Now, I am filled with the Holy Spirit. The Holy Spirit is leading me into righteous and truth. The Holy Spirit is with me every day guiding me to God's success.

(John 14:17, 14.26, 15:26, 16,18, 16:13,15; Acts 1:16. 2 Peter 1:21. Acts 8:29; I Corinthians 2:10-13; Romans 15:30; 1 Corinthians 12:11; Romans 8:27).

Matthew 15:8 (NIV) *"These people honor me with their lips, but their hearts are far from me."*

The prophet Isaiah criticized hypocrites (Isaiah 29:13 NIV, *"13 The Lord says: "These people come near to me with their mouth and honor me with their lips, but their hearts are far from me. Their worship of me is based on merely human rules they have been taught."*) and Jesus applied Isaiah's words to these religious leaders. The Pharisees knew a lot about God, but they did not know God. Attitudes and motives determine your success. Before 2010 setbacks, I understood a lot about God. I knew to go to church, pay my tithes and offerings, and to love others. With a blink of the eye, my heart stumbled to the point where I was more concerned with making money, than the things of God. Instead of God's success in the first business adventure; the model of success was making money. I did all the outer things of God by showing a smile, by going to church, and so forth. Although, my household and business was not in order.

At this point of my life, "success" is having a successful relationship with God and stability in my marriage, family, church, and business. Money had taken the place of my marriage, loving my husband, and finding pleasure in spending time with my family. Do not get me mistaken. **My Love was genuine to All.**

I always understood the importance of marriage. Therefore, my marriage was the first thing the devil attacked. However, I still managed to put a smile on my face like everything in my household was fabulous. After many attacks of the enemy in my marriage, without the source; God. I no longer found success in my marriage; therefore, I was not able to put my heart into my business. Also, due to the despondency in my marriage, I did some things that were out of the will of God that effected my marriage and family. Say "But God"……..**But God!**, gave me another opportunity to make it right.

Through the process, I have learned how to have the **JOY of the Lord in my heart!** "……..*for the joy of the Lord is your strength."* Nehemiah 8:10 (KJV). In spite of the challenges that life brings, you cannot claim to honor God while your heart is far from him.

When your heart is far from Him, your worship and success means nothing. Your inner and outer actions need to link up with the Word of God. You need to be heartfelt with your actions and your attitude. You have to continuously remove those inner thoughts and actions that are hindering you from your future success. Your actions and your attitude are part of your heart and they must be sincere, to receive the success of God.

Matthew 15:18-20 (NKJV) *"18 But those things which proceed out of the mouth come from the heart, and they defile a man. 19 For out of the heart proceed evil thoughts, murders, adulteries, fornications, thefts, false witness, blasphemies. 20 These are the things which defile a man, but to eat with unwashed hands does not defile a man."*

Healthy thoughts, attitudes, and motives are success; not healthy food, exercise, homes, cars, jewelry, and so forth. You work hard to look attractive on the outside. God is more concerned with the inside of you; which is your heart. What is planted deep down inside of you is what the world cannot see; it's what God sees. When people become Christians, God makes them different on the inside; not the outside. Success is in your heart; the inner part of your body. My God!...... My God!.......Success starts in the heart. Your outer appearance only pleases the world success.

The inner appearance gratifies God.

Matthew 23:26 (NIV) *"Blind Pharisee! First clean the inside of the cup and dish, and then the outside will be clean."*

Once again, your outward appearance may appear to be saintly and holy; but inward is full of corruption and greed. Deliverance and healing had to take place in order for me to be set free from all the anger, frustration, hurt, pain, bad relationships, disappointments, laziness, hatefulness, unforgiveness, ... from inside of me that had built up in 2010. The process is called "cleansing" which is repenting of the wrong/sinful actions in your life.

Exercise 4: List your known corruption and greed.

1. Adultery   6._____   11._____

2. Money   7._____   12._____

3. Rage   8._____   13._____

4. Fornication   9._____   14. Land

5._____   10._____   15. Fame

Once you have identified your known corruption and greed, speak to your heart. **"Heart, I no longer want to be full of corruption and greed, I decree and declare cleanliness and pureness in my heart, in Jesus name. Amen!"** Now, since you have been set free and cleansed on the inside; now your cleanliness on the outside will not be a sham.

(Read Mark 7:1-23 for further insight)

Notes from Mark 7:1-23

_____
_____
_____
_____
_____
_____
_____

Romans 2:14-16 (NIV) *"14 (Indeed, when Gentiles, who do not have the law, do by nature things required by the law, they are a law for themselves, even though they do not have the law. 15 They show that the requirements of the law are written on their hearts, their consciences also bearing witness, and their thoughts sometimes accusing them and at other times even defending them.) 16 This will take place on the day when God judges people's secrets through Jesus Christ, as my gospel declares."*

I always questioned, "what if people do not know the Word of God" or "know right from wrong". God showed me in the scripture above that there is no excuse for not doing right or doing wrong. Romans 2:14-16 states that people are condemned not for what they do not know, but for what they do with what they know.

Everybody has a conscience that tells them if they are doing something right or wrong. **I repeat, everyone has a conscience. No exceptions!** *Therefore, those who know the Word of God will be judged by them.*

But, those who have never seen a Bible will be judged because they did not keep the standards of their own consciences; for right and wrong. Therefore, everyone is destined for success.

Admit to God that you fit the human pattern of God's standard or conscience standard. Ask God for forgiveness of all wrongdoing. Ask for forgiveness so you can be delivered, healed and set free.

Now you can change your mindset from conscience standards to studying God's standards, His Word; so that you can live a prosperous and successful fulfilled life.

Psalm 51:10 (NIV) *"Create in me a pure heart, O God, and renew a steadfast spirit within me."*

You must first come to grips that we were all born as sinners (Psalms 51:5 KJV *"Behold, I was shapen in iniquity; and in sin did my mother conceive me"*.) You were born to please yourself and your flesh, instead of God. David followed his desires and his flesh. Also, another man's wife. Like David is asking, you must ask God to cleanse you from within (Psalms 51:7 KJV *"Purge me with hyssop, and I shall be clean; wash me, and I shall be whiter than snow"* .) Ask God to clean your heart and spirit for new thoughts and desires.

Only the right conduct that leads to success, in God, comes from a clean heart and a steadfast spirit. I did some things that were out of the "will of God" in my marriage. Once I really turned my life back over to God, I asked him to remove those sins and create in me a clean and pure heart. Remember, you have to ask God daily for his purification and cleansing. Its not a once a week cleansing and purification; it is a daily process. We all sin on a daily basis one way or another. Let's make it a habit to ask God every morning, when you awake, to clean and purify your heart.

Part of your morning prayer should be *"God create in me a pure heart and a steadfast spirit in me."*

Watch how the Holy Spirit leads and guides you into success. Commit to your memory that success is a **"choice"**. Also, learn by heart that you have to acknowledge to God that you have sinful acts and you are asking for his cleansing and purification before you start your day.

Psalm 51:17 (NIV) *"The sacrifices of God are a broken spirit, A broken and a contrite heart—These, O God, You will not despise."*

1 Kings 3:11-12 (NIV) *"11 So God said to him, "Since you have asked for this and not for long life or wealth for yourself, nor have asked for the death of your enemies but for discernment in administering justice, 12 I will do what you have asked. I will give you a wise and discerning heart, so that there will never have been anyone like you, nor will there ever be."*

Solomon did not ask for wealth, he asked for wisdom and discernment to lead the people. Therefore, God gave him more than he asked for; and he added him riches and long life. God does not promise riches to all that follow him, but he gives you wisdom to put his kingdom, his interests and his principles first. Wealth is not success. Wealth and richness is good on earth; but you will always want more because you still will not be satisfied. It is a known fact that we will always want more. It is not that you are not content with what you have. It is that we try to keep up with the trend. You want to update your car, your clothes, your shoes, and even your zip code. But, when you set your heart on the things of God, then he can satisfy your deepest needs. With a wise and discerning heart from God, you can apply wisdom to all areas of your life.

You can apply wisdom in your marriage, raising your children, concerning your health, on your job, business investments, and life challenges. **WE** all need God's wisdom in all the areas of our life to keep us balanced, less stressful, and more successful.

God Knows Your Heart

Deuteronomy 31:21 (NIV) *"And when many disasters and calamities come on them, this song will testify against them, because it will not be forgotten by their descendants. I know what they are disposed to do, even before I bring them into the land I promised them on oath."*

God already knows your heart; because he created you in his own image. He knows the what, when and where of your heart. God told Moses in Deuteronomy 31:21 what they are **disposed** to do; even before He brought them into the land he promised them on oath. The definition of disposed – "is to place or set in a particular order; arrange or having made preparations, or prepared to take risks". God has already made the preparations to carry out His plan in your life. I was always told that God doesn't bring you to anything that he cannot bring you out of. God is just seeking "willing" helpers/servants to carry out His plans; not our plans. God already knows our skills and abilities that dwells on the inside of us. God already knows that you are successful, before you even thought you could be successful. Jesus! Jesus! **WE ARE SUCCESSFUL!**

1 Samuel 16:7 (NIV) *" But the Lord said to Samuel, "Do not consider his appearance or his height, for I have rejected him. The Lord does not look at the things people look at. People look at the outward appearance, but the Lord looks at the heart."*

God does not consider outer appearance, but the heart He judges. Samuel was looking for the next king for Israel. Saul was a tall and handsome man. It appears that Samuel was looking for the same appearances and qualities of Saul. But, God stated that he looks at the heart; not the appearance or height.

In 1 Samuel 16:8-12, Jesse had 7 sons that appeared to be of high statues. But, they didn't pass the test of the Lord. It was David, the one that was tending the sheep that passed the test. Most important, David was already in position. "ACTION". He was tending to the sheep, when he was called. David was already working and was busy. God loves busy people. God judges by faith and character; not appearances.

God is looking for individuals that are cashiers at the local grocery store; without a high school diploma. They may not have a high school diploma, but at least they are working towards something; because they already have a job. God is looking for that single mother or father that has 4 kids and lives in a one bedroom apartment; but already have their hearts set on being that successful business owner one day. That single mother or father already has their business plans written.

In addition, the single mother or father spending the many hours researching for the right location for their office. I have been told that it's the people that have endured much hurt, pain and hardship that make success a high calling from God. (Samuel anoints David as king; 1 Samuel 16:1-23). Therefore, the hurt, pain, and hardship are to make you stronger and wiser; for His success. God places us in humble places. When I was making the millions, I thought I didn't have to humble myself before God. Why? I had the home, cars and money. Matthew 6:19-21 ESV *"19 "Do not lay up for yourselves treasures on earth, where moth and rust destroy and where thieves break in and steal, 20 but lay up for yourselves treasures in heaven, where neither moth nor rust destroys and where thieves do not break in and steal. 21 For where your treasure is, there your heart will be also."* There is nothing wrong with wealth, but you need to understand the difference between material wealth and spiritual wealth. I was fixed on earthly wealth; instead of spiritual wealth.

I always knew God blessed me, but I did not have that everyday consistent prayer life with God. 1Thessalonians 5:17 (KJV) *"Pray without ceasing."* God gave me much, but I did not give him much of me back. In order to get that full feeling of satisfaction, you need to find spiritual wealth. Spiritual wealth is about riches, not money. What kinds of riches? Romans 11:33 (NIV) *"Oh, the depth of the riches of the wisdom and knowledge of God! How unsearchable his judgments, and his paths beyond tracing out!"* The following chinese proverb can shed some light on the difference between material and spiritual wealth:

Money can buy you a house but not a home.
Money can buy you a bed but not sleep.
Money can buy you medicine but not health.
Money can buy you blood but not life.
Money can buy you a lover but not love.
Money can buy you amusements but not happiness.
Money can buy you books but not wisdom.
Money can buy you a clock but not more time.
Money can buy you companions but not real friends.
Money can buy you food but not an appetite.
Money can buy you a ring but not a marriage.

Spiritual wealth is something much more significant than material wealth. **Spiritual wealth is the route to pure "JOY".** But how can a person cultivate a sense of spiritual wealth? It's simple enough to become materially wealthy, but spiritual wealth is something different.

It takes patience, self-discipline and strength to become a spiritually wealthy person.

Solomon prayer to God of Dedication

1 Kings 8:39 (NIV) *"then hear from heaven, your dwelling place. Forgive and act; deal with everyone according to all they do, since you know their hearts (for you alone know every human heart,)"*

All the toiling has been done through our forefathers. Solomon has already released a powerful prayer for our success; when our hearts are on one accord with God and the things of God. Once I realize that I really had God on the inside of me, I began to reflect and mediate on the things of God. Now, I can say to God, **"Thank you God for forgiving me and putting me back on the right track to success. You know my heart. Thank you for dealing with me according to my heart. Success is where I want to be. But, I cannot do it without you. In Jesus name. Amen."** Since, you know God deals with the heart according, your heart needs to be set on the things of God. When your heart is on one accord with the things of God, then you can easily say **"thank you"** in advance after you pray. Pray according to his purpose for your life. Then, say "thank you" in advance, before it has been given to you, because you know your heart is in position to receive. Jesus! When you ask and then thank Him in advance, you are confirming to God, that you trust that he will give you what you ask; according to His will and purpose for your life.

1 Kings 8:15-21 (NIV) *15 Then he said: "Praise be to the Lord, the God of Israel, who with his own hand has fulfilled what he promised with his own mouth to my father David. For he said, 16 'Since the day I brought my people Israel out of Egypt, I have not chosen a city in any tribe of Israel to have a temple built so that my Name might be there, but I have chosen David to rule my people Israel.' 17 "My father David had it in his heart to build a temple for the Name of the Lord, the God of Israel. 18 But the Lord said to my father David, 'You did well to have it in your heart to build a temple for my Name. 19 Nevertheless, you are not the one to build the temple, but your son, your own flesh*

and blood—he is the one who will build the temple for my Name.' 20 "The Lord has kept the promise he made: I have succeeded David my father and now I sit on the throne of Israel, just as the Lord promised, and I have built the temple for the Name of the Lord, the God of Israel. 21 I have provided a place there for the ark, in which is the covenant of the Lord that he made with our ancestors when he brought them out of Egypt."

You no longer have to look at the size of a church building to determine your success. 1 Kings 8 states "it is not the size of the temple, but the size of a man's heart". Even when it comes to owning a business. It is not the size of the corporate building, it is the size of the heart of the owners. I have always assumed, I needed this seven office building to run a successful company. I came into contact with some owners that operates a million dollar landscaping company out of their homes. The owners I came in contact with, really, loves the Lord. They even mention to me during their employees lunch hours, their employees read their bible.

Also, my husband worked for a very successful company. The owners conducted the company's business out of their home. So, do not think that you need an office building to start your successful business. Work with what you have until God opens the door with what is needed to continue operation.

1 Chronicles 28:9 (CEB) *"9 As for you, Solomon, my son, acknowledge your father's God and serve him with enthusiastic devotion, because the Lord searches every mind and understands the motive behind every thought. If you seek him, he will be found by you; but if you abandon him, he will reject you forever.."*

David told his son, Solomon, to acknowledge the God of your father and serve him with all your heart. What is being said is that you cannot trick God? Our motives should be for things of God and providing for His kingdom. If you are successful in eating healthy and losing 50lbs, share with someone else how you achieved that goal. I know every child is different in the personality area. But, if you see a parent that is having difficult with their child's behavior, give them some of your tips in being successful with handling disciplinary problems. Find out what the community needs. Does your local church need volunteers in the food pantry or clothes ministry? Is there a widow in your neighborhood that needs their yard cut? Can you buy a family of five (5) bags of groceries this week? Our success is for others to come to know God and his goodness. God is "love."

If your neighbor sees you doing good deeds, then they will want to know…. who you know!

I can remember when I first understood God and success. I started feeding the homeless people at the Jacksonville Landing in Jacksonville, Florida. Then, God assigned me to a young man on the streets that I had to make sure he had breakfast and dinner everyday.

I was successful with those, I thought, small assignments. Now, God has placed me in a church where I volunteer on Tuesday's to help distribute food items to over 40 people weekly. I made the initiative to feed the homeless at the Jacksonville Landing. I was faithful in feeding a young man for months, now over 40 people weekly. Look at God! My heart motive and passion is to help the homeless and the less fortune people.

If you do not have a heart motive, God has several motives in the Bible. The one that is heavenly on my heart is in *Deuteronomy 15:7 -8 (NIRV)* *"7 Suppose there are poor people among you. And suppose they live in one of the towns in the land the Lord your God is giving you. Then don't be mean to them. They are poor. So don't hold back money from them. 8 Instead, open your hands and lend them what they need. Do it freely."*

Luke 3:11 (NASB) "11 And he would answer and say to them, "The man who has two tunics is to share with him who has none; and he who has food is to do likewise."

My family and I lived with my father for two and half years in Jacksonville, Florida. Almost on every corner of the City of Jacksonville, Florida are homeless people. Therefore, I make it my priority to find a homeless person that needs something to eat.

(You can contact your local police department to find out where to go feed the homeless in your area.)

I can remember riding around with a couple of sandwiches, bananas and water in my car. When I saw a homeless person, I just pulled over and gave them a meal. I involved my kids in this process, as well. I was not employed at the time, but God made a way for me to purchase the necessary food items. When God knows your heart is for His people, He will make provision for you to give.

Proverbs 19:17 (NASB) states *"One who is gracious to a poor man lends to the Lord, And He will repay him for his good deed.."* All you successful business owners should choose to give a portion of your success earnings back to Gods' people....

Colossians 2:18 (NIV) *" Do not let anyone who delights in false humility and the worship of angels disqualify you. Such a person also goes into great detail about what they have seen; they are puffed up with idle notions by their unspiritual mind."*

Allow God's Word to guide you; not people. There will be many conversations about the Bible, and the way of God, on your journey to becoming successful. You have to **study** the Word yourself to **know** the Word of God. If you are not in an agreement with someone concerning the Word, just silence yourself. (Proverbs 17:28 (ESV).

"Even a fool who keeps silent is considered wise; when he closes his lips, he is deemed delight". Actually, you do not have to agree or disagree; just silence yourself. (Exodus 14:14 (ESV)*"The Lord will fight for you, and you have only to be silent"*) With silence, there cannot be an argument or debate. I am not saying, do not believe what people are saying to you; because some people give good advice.

Although, some people just give their opinions. There are many people that will try to come and distract you because of your success. If I am not familiar with what someone is saying concerning my life or my future, I just listen with silence; then later go back and find a scripture for clarification. I know what God has for me. I love all kinds of advice; even constructive criticism. If I have not read the scripture or know the biblical story of a statement, I silence myself. I do not say "yes or no" nor "agree or disagree." I write down the scriptures myself so I can seek God for revelation. What people speak is very important. Words are powerful. You do not need anyone speaking something that is not of God into your ears. Avoid these types of people and keep them in your prayers. (Luke 6:28 (NIV) *"bless those who curse you, pray for those who mistreat you."*)

Numbers 23:19 (NIV) *"God is not a man, that he should lie, not a human being, that he should change his mind. Does he speak and hen not act? Does he promise and not fulfill?"*

Balak took Balaam to several places to try to entice him to curse the Israelites. Because of some insecurities and not feeling important at this one particular church, I did depart from the church without God's permission in Jacksonville, Florida in 2012. Because I left the church out of the will of God, I ended up in a church where I saw witchcraft and other evil activities. Instantaneously, I returned to the church I left. I made amends and received more healing. After a few months being back at the church, I was released from the church.

Once again, instead of me seeking God's approval in my Mind, I was seeking man's approval at the church. This little process of me departing and returning made my situation a little bit harder. Not only did I not feel important anymore; the trials in my marriage got a little bit harder, at one point, wanting to give up. God puts us in certain places and situations for a reason. I was at this church to learn how to pray, to serve and to love my husband; not to make friends or feel important. A change of church, resident, job or location may only distract us from the purpose of God. Stay in your position, wherever you are until God has finished molding and transforming you into greater, then He will move you.

In addition, once I returned back to the church, I sat my hips down from ushering, praying out loud, announcements, and so on. I had hurt a lot of the members in the church because of my own selfish desires. When I returned, I did feel some isolation. The attention was no longer on me. Because my husband was not showing me the affection that I needed, I got caught up in my emotions. Imagine that feeling when you think there is no love at home or the church. My God! My God! My God! I realized through these experiences that the husband nor the church can love me the way God is capable of. Still, through this little emotional roller coaster, I still stood on the promises of God; that **"I will be restored spiritually, emotionally, physically, mentally, and financially."**

I did not move again, until I was completely healed of church hurt, marriage hurt, and family hurt. I did not care if I did not traveled anymore with the church. I did not care if my husband did not show me love.

I did not care if my family thought I was fanatical for staying in my marriage. All that mattered was that my "Mind" was set on the things of God, which required "loving God with all my heart, soul and mind." After I was released from the church that Sunday evening by a phone call, that same week Monday. I had replied to an email to volunteer at a food pantry for that following Saturday at Helping Hands Depot, Inc, I answered a month ago. Let me tell you how God works. When I answered the ad a month ago, for some reason, the event was cancelled. But, I had received an email that week after I was released to see if I was still interesting in volunteer. Look at God! (The timing was already in place.) I volunteered that Saturday. Because of the warmth and generosity of the volunteers toward the people of the community that were being served, I wanted to know what church they were attending. The food pantry is sponsored by Guiding Light Ministries, Inc., two doors from the food pantry. Furthermore, I attended the church the next day, Sunday, and been there since October 2012. God set me up for a blessing. Because of my willing to go back to the church I had left, to make amends, and to receive my healing; God opened some doors for me.

In this season of ministry, God is using me to pray and speak prophetically to the church, feed the needy, teach Sunday school, and anything else that is required of me at the church and in the community. *"God is not a man, that he should lie, nor a son of man, that he should change his mind."* My promises are being fulfilled. Allow God to guide you in the preparation stage to your success.

Your thoughts at this moment:

_____
_____
_____
_____
_____
_____
_____
_____
_____
_____
_____
_____
_____
_____
_____
_____

Chapter Three

THE SOUL

Revelation 6:9 (NIV) *"When he opened the fifth seal, I saw under the altar the souls of those who had been slain because of the word of God and testimony they had maintained."*

John saw the souls of martyrs who had died for preaching the gospel. In the face of warfare, famine, persecution, and death; Christians will be "called on" to stand firmly for what they believe. Only those who endure to the end will be rewarded by God. Mark 13:13 (NIV) *"Everyone will hate you because of me, but the one who stands firm to the end will be saved."*

It may have looked like my business may have shattered to pieces in the sight of my enemies. Although I sinned and did wrong, God gave me another chance to get it "right." Due to all the pain and suffering, I know I was called to do "Great" things. Yes, God blessed me tremendously in my first business adventure, but my soul was worshipping other gods; such as, "money" and "adultery". God used these little gods to show me who the real big God is. Yes, I have gone through much persecution since 2010, because of the love I have for Jesus and God. Through it all, God has made me stronger.

I could have easily stayed in my mess and worshiped these little gods, but there would have been no eternal reward, which is heaven!

I want my testimony to speak, "The businesses are successful because God is in control of my heart, mind and soul," "I stayed faithful to God, " "I stayed faithful to my marriage," and "I am a Great wife, mother and friend to many".   Also, "I am a good steward of money for God's kingdom." I do not want to give any credit to man nor these little gods. **My soul is for the things of God and only God!**

Lamentations 3:27-33 (NIV) *"27 It is good for a man to bear the yoke while he is young. 28 Let him sit alone in silence, for the Lord has laid it on him. 29 Let him bury his face in the dust—there may yet be hope. 30 Let him offer his cheek to one who would strike him, and let him be filled with disgrace. 31 For no one is cast off by the Lord forever. 32 Though he brings grief, he will show compassion, so great is his unfailing love. 33 For he does not willingly bring affliction or grief to anyone."*

To bear the yoke means to "willingly" come under God's discipline and to learn what he wants to teach you concerning your success. The way to get Gods attention is to:

1. Silent reflection on what God wants.

2. Repent humility.

3. Self control in the face of adversity.

4. Confidence and patience.

5. Depend on the divine Teacher to bring about loving lessons in your lives for success.

Jesus said that loving God with all ourselves is the first and greatest commandment (Matthew 22:37-39).

How do we do this?

1. Love God with power and might.

2. Love God in spite of your circumstances or situations.

3. Love God through your trials and tribulations.

4. Love God every second of the day.

5. Just Love God!

2 Kings 23:25 (NIV) *"Neither before not after Josiah was there a king like him who turned to the Lord as he did-with all his heart and with all his soul and with all his strength, in accordance with all the Law of Moses."*

Josiah is remembered as Judah's most obedient king. Once I started following in obedience, then I was able to follow this pattern for God's success and kingdom business:

1. He/she (me) recognized sin.

2. He/she (me) eliminated sinful practices.

3. He/she (me) attacked the causes of sin.

The three above approaches worked for me when temptations and enticements surfaced. Not only must you remove sinful actions, you must eliminate the causes of sin. I eliminated my sins by removing myself from situations, relationships, routines, and patterns of life that led me to the door of temptation.

Recognition of Sin

I experienced a depression stage at one point in my life. I found myself consuming a lot of alcohol when I went out to dinner and gatherings. I tried to respect my home and my children, therefore, a lot of my consuming of alcohol was done outside of the home. When I went out to places like TGIF, Chili's and Buffalo Wings, I consumed margaritas. When I decided to give my life back to God, I did not go near these places for a meal; until I was fully delivered.

1.) I recognized the sin: drinking margarita's.

2.) Eliminated the sinful practices: I repented and asked for forgiveness; then ask God for help.

3.) Attacked the causes of sin: I no longer went to restaurants or places that had bars or drinks to entice me on the menu. To be honest, it was just about every restaurant in town. I was serious about removing this addiction from my life. Additionally, I had to start back cooking. From time to time, we enjoyed eating at fast food restaurants or buffet style restaurants.

After I was delivered from the enticements and temptations of margarita's and all alcoholic beverages, maybe six months.

(**Note:** I stopped consuming alcohol immediately, it was the enticements and temptations that hung around; the residue of alcohol.) Then, I was able to enjoy my favorite restaurants. Now, when I am at those favorite restaurants temptations still comes knocking; but, I say right then and there at the table, "The devil is a liar, Satan I rebuke you!" Immediately the temptations leaves. I am no longer bound to alcoholic beverages. Thank you, Jesus!

(I try and make it a point not to judge other Christians who drink or who abstain from drinking. We are "free" as Christians to do many things, but not all things are profitable (1Cor.6:12). We have tremendous leeway in how we live our lives (Gal.5:1), but the whole point of our lives is to serve our Master and His Body, the Church (1Cor.10:23-24).)

Proverbs 31:4-5 9 (NIV) *"4 It is not for kings, Lemuel—it is not for kings to drink wine, not for rulers to crave beer, 5 lest they drink and forget what has been decreed, and deprive all the oppressed of their rights."*

Elimination of Sin….

-Why hang out after work with the guys when you know they are going to have bottles of beer waiting for you?

-Why go to Auntie Liz house when you know she has a bar in the basement?

-Change the way you come home from work. Why pass down Main Street by the liquor store when you can take James street home?

Eliminate Routines of Sin...

-Stop sitting at the bar of a restaurant.

-Stop going to family gatherings or social events when you know that side of the family consumed alcohol, heavily. My family did not understand why I was not attending many family gatherings. I did not share with anyone what was going on. I was trying to get delivered with God's help; not man's help.

I did not need anyone placing me in the spotlight saying, "Eureka is trying to stop drinking alcohol, let's not give her a drink tonight". Because they know they are not ready to stop some bad habits; there is always that family member or friend that will put your business in the spotlight. I have learned when you are trying to stop a bad habit, do not tell anyone, just seek God and allow him to show you "how".

In 2 Kings 23:1-20, Josiah realized the terrible state of Judah's religious life, he did something about it. You can say what you are going to do, but your action speaks louder than words. When you respond to action; you are doing what faith requires. This means acting differently at home, church, school, work, and community.

Josiah's father and grandfather were wicked. His life is an example of God's willingness to provide ongoing guidance to those who set out to be obedient. At an young age, Josiah understood that there was spiritual sickness in his land. There was much idol worshiping. Josiah began to search for God by destroying and cleaning up whatever he recognized as not belonging to the worship of God.

In the process, God's Word was rediscovered.

The king's intentions and the power of God's written revelation were brought together.

1. Josiah renews the Covenant (which, was found in the temple of the Lord)

2. Removed all the articles made for Baal and Asherah, starry hosts.

3. Burned the outside Kidron Valley and took ashes to Bethel.

4. Did away with pagan priests appointed by kings to Judah, who burned incense on the high places of Judah and around Jerusalem----those who burned incense to Baal, the sun, the moon, constellations and starry hosts.

5. Took Asherah pole from the temple of the Lord, the Kidron Valley, outside Jerusalem and burned it there.

6. Tore down the quarters of male shrine prostitutes. Also, where the women were weaving for Asherah.

7. Bought all the priests of Judah and desecrated the high places, from Geba to Beersheba where the priests had burned incense.

8. Broken down the shrines gates.

If Josiah can reorganize the temple, why can't you reorganize your temple (your body; the soul, heart and mind) for God's success. In my next business adventure, I will reorganize my operating structure based on God's Word. Because I was once lost in wrongdoings as a business owner, I will never judge anyone or point out sins; although, my business will have some godly guidelines to adhere by. I have been restored through our Lord and Savior, Jesus Christ. My goal is not to change anyone, but to show them righteousness and holiness through my lifestyle. Additionally, there are certain biblical practices that I will put in place to make sure God's business remains successful. I have learned through my journey of restoration, that if I have to live right, my employees are going to live the same lifestyle.

Your business will be for the God's kingdom. Your business should be based on biblical principles. Some of the questions that should be on your interview checklist are: Do you pay your tithe and offering? (Then you will not have to worry about anyone asking for a loan.) What is your ministry in the church?....feeding the homeless, ushering, hospitality committee, and so forth on. (Then you will know the interviewee has respect for people's feelings and have a caring heart.)

Through Obedience....

Psalm 23:2-3 (NKJV) *"2 He makes me to lie down in green pastures; He leads me beside the still waters. 3: He restores my soul; He leads me in the paths of righteousness For His name's sake."*

When you allow God, your shepherd to guide you in success, you are showing contentment. You will reach the places of "green pastures" and "quiet/still waters" that will restore you. Never let **one** failed business stop you from reaching and climbing for it again. Never let one failed marriage stop you from remarrying. Never let one bad grade in school stop you from continuing your education. Rebelling against God's leadership is actually rebelling against your own best interest. God already has your life plan in order. On your next success launch, you must remember to put your soul into God's way of action. Ask for his guidance so that you will be led to "green pastures" by the "quiet/still waters."

Psalm 42:1-2 (NIV) *"1 As the deer pants for streams of water, so my soul pants for you, O God. 2 My soul thirsts for God, for the living God. When can I go and meet with God?"*

As a little deer is dependent upon water, whereas; your life, lifestyle, marriage, relationships, and businesses must depend upon God. Those who seek him and long to understand him, find never-ending life and everlasting success. Like the deer ponders for water until found, so should your souls seek God until you are fulfilled and thirst no more.

Psalm 42:11 (NIV) *"Why are you downcast, O my soul? Why so disturbed within me? Put your hope in God, for I will yet praise him, my Savior and my God."*

Put all Hope in God. Put your marriage in God's hope, your children in God's hope, your business in God's hope, your job in God's hope,........ God is saying, "Why are you downcast or disturbed?" There is no reason for downcast or disturbed types of actions. WE no longer have to feel dejected, anxious, sad, disappointed, discouraged, troubled or worried. All you have to do is Hope in him, your God; not man. God is just seeking your obedience and willingness in him.

Psalm 62:5 (NIV) *"Find rest, O my Soul, in God alone; my hope comes from him."*

When your soul is resting in God, nothing or anyone can hurt you. A set back in a marriage, a setback in your business, a setback on the job, or a setback concerning some bad choices your children made; you can still find hope that comes from God. Remember setbacks have comebacks. Let us make our comeback in the Hope of God. From this day forward, speak, "my soul rests in God forever!" Psalm 62:6 (NIV) *"He alone is my rock and my salvation; he is my fortress, I will never be shaken."*

God is my ALL. God is my Rock. God is my Salvation. God is my Fortress.................God is my everything; even in the time of testing and trials that occurs in my marriage, family, businesses, and relationships.

"GOD ALONE IS MY ROCK"

Proverbs 13:19 (NIV) *"A longing fulfilled is sweet to the soul, but fools detest turning from evil."*

"Longing fulfilled" is a tree of life. "Longing fulfilled" is "Hope" that cherish a desire with anticipation, expectation and confidence. "Longing fulfilled" is "sweet to the soul" that achieve worthwhile goals. Again, all goals are worth pursuing. When you set your heart on something, you may not assess it with good nature. Sometimes your desires blind your judgment. Sometimes your desires may allow you to be in an unwise relationships, a wasteful purchase, accepting a job based on pay; although, not enjoying the work of the job, making poor business investment, and so on. You might ask a few questions yourself before making a decision on a "longing fulfilled" goal.

Exercise 5: Longing Fulfilled

(You may have to plug in a long term goal to answer the questions below.)

Long term goal:
_____
_____
_____

1. On your current job, do you smile and speak nice to your co-workers? _____

2. Do you still treat your boss with respect when they are wrong? _____

3. Do you wake up every morning joyful to go to your place of work? _____

4. Do you give hugs and hand shanks when you feed the hungry? _____

5. How does your business ideas line up with God's plan for the homeless, widows, and orphans   (James 1:27)?
_____
_____
_____
_____

6. Do you tithe your job income or business income? _____

Exercise 6: The Soul Search for Success

Follow the instructions in this order:

1. Grab a pencil or pen and some paper.

2. Find a quiet spot, in the bathroom, if necessary.

3. Make a list of problems and hinges that is hindering you from succeeding.

4. If you get stuck, think of why you have not been on that dream cruise, why you cannot fit into that dress that you bought a year ago, and so forth on.? Has anyone asked you for advice on something lately and you were not able to answer them because you are having the same problem; but you haven not shared it with anyone???

5. After you have listed as many problems you can think of, go back over your list and think of solutions to the problems. Always remember every problem has a solution.

6. Go over the list and prioritized which ones need to be eliminated today. Put number "1" by those.

7. Then, put a number "2" by the ones that can be eliminated within a week.

8. Now, the ones that are remaining means it will take some time to overcome. That is okay. You want to work hard on the most difficult challenges first.

9. Put the list away for a week.

10. After the week, go back and look over your list in your quiet space and prioritized your numbers, again…."STOP"…. before reading on………… look over your list.

11. If your numbers 1, 2 have changed in their order, then, you have been doing some soul searching. God has intervened. God has began a healing process in you. Your deliverance is about to take place. God already knows your problems, but you had to be honest with yourself before God can do the work in you.

Your feedback.

_____
_____
_____
_____
_____
_____
_____
_____
_____
_____
_____
                    _____

Chapter Four

The Mind

The more you think about something, the stronger it takes hold of you; which is why the Bible teaches that you should, *"Run from anything that gives you the evil thoughts . . . but stay close to anything that makes you want to do right."* (2 Timothy 2:22 LB). Temptation begins by capturing your attention. What gets your attention arouses your emotions. Then, your emotions activate your behavior and you act on what you felt. The more you focus on "I don't want to do this," the stronger it draws you into its web. Ignoring a temptation is far more effective than fighting it. Once your mind is on something else, the temptation loses its power. So when temptation calls you on the phone, don't argue with it, just hang up! Sometimes this means physically leaving a tempting situation. This is one time it is okay to run away. Get up and turn off the television set. Walk away from a group that is gossiping. Leave the theater in the middle of the movie. **To avoid being stung, stay away from the bees**. Do whatever is necessary to turn your attention to something else.

Spiritually, your mind is your most vulnerable organ. To reduce temptation, keep your mind occupied with God's Word; and other good and perfect thoughts. You defeat bad thoughts by thinking of something better. This is the "principle of replacement". Romans 12:21 (KJV)*"Be not overcome of evil, but overcome evil with good."*

Satan can not get your attention when your mind is preoccupied with something else that is good and perfect. That's why the Bible repeatedly tells us to keep our minds focused: *"..........fix your thoughts on Jesus, ..."* (Hebrews 3:1 NIV).

"In conclusion, my friends, fill your minds with those things that are good and that deserve praise: things that are true, noble, right, pure, lovely, and honorable." Philippians 4:8 GNT. If you're serious about defeating temptation, you must manage your mind, monitor your media intake, and be discerning of your environment. The wisest man who ever lived warned, *"Be careful how you think; your life is shaped by your thoughts."* (Proverbs 4:23 GNT).

Church hurt is the worst hurt anyone can endure. Once I started listening more to God, I understood why some actions had to take place. One main action was being released from a church. When this happened, I really and totally put all my focus and trust in God. If God tells me to go back to the church, I will. I thought I was truly working things out with the leaders and receiving the trust level back. Not understanding the full extent of the release could have caused me to miss out on my blessings. The release was God really telling me it was time for me to move forward. My season at that ministry was fulfilled. The leader fulfilled her role by holding me close to her, until I was healed of some past hurts and wounds. God used her to build my self-esteem back up. After speaking with several people, I was told no leader presume to release anyone without knowing where they are going. Normally, a person asks for release when they join another church. In my situation, this was different. It was my time of elevation, which meant departing from the church.

Once, I was able to allow the hurt of being release from a church depart from my spirit, I was able to hear God clearly concerning what He had in store for me and my family. One day as I was meditating, my mother dropped heavily in my Spirit. I told God, "my mother put a lot of responsibilities on me." There are things that I have not shared with anyone that my mother spoke to me; concerning my sisters. I believe I did my part as a sister; for my sisters. One of my sisters has her own successful business and the other sister has a successful career as an educator. Therefore, my mom's influence in me has paid off for them. Now it's time for me to receive my Greater! My mother understood me more than anyone. I would talk to her all times of the hours; midnight, 3am and even 5am in the mornings. Since my mother passing, no one else can get that close to me. Once they try, I do something to make them not trust me. God is saying to me, "don't get close to anyone because I have work for you to do."

I realized quickly; God is my only source; comforter and provider. God only wants my heart, soul and mind on him. But, it was on a Saturday in 2012, I went to a volunteer for an assignment at Helping Hands Depot, Inc. Met the leaders. Went to the church that Sunday, the day afterwards. Its 2013, I am still at the ministry and working in the ministry. This feel like a Paul and Apollo's anointing. Learn how to fast at Agape Fellowship Center, Quincy, Florida. Learn how to pray at Anointed Word Christian Center, Jacksonville, Florida. Working in the ministry at Guiding Light Ministries, Inc, Jacksonville, Florida. Even though I didn't feel the same return of assistance and help from people when my business closed. That was okay. The non assistance made me depend more on God.

God wants full credit for all he is doing in my family and my life. Now, it is time for me to gain this spiritual wealth that I have been "longing fulfilled." With spiritual wealth, I can manage the many projects that God has in store for my family and I. I have suffered much. I have fasted and prayed for my next level in God; spiritually, physically, emotionally, and financially. Many leaders have pushed me into my destiny. Many of God's promises through prophecy have been fulfilled. The Word says in Numbers 23:19 (NIV)..."*God is not human, that he should lie, not a human being, that he should change his mind. Does he speak and then not act? Does he promise and not fulfill?*"

I can thank God over and over again for just being God. I can speak, "**I am Blessed and Highly Favored!**" I know that God's ministry is in my husband and I. Lord, thank you for saving my marriage for ministry! Thank you for your mercy, grace and favor!

Use this space to write down your thoughts and reactions:

_____
_____
_____
_____
_____
_____
_____

Exercise 7: Success Mindset

Fill in the Blanks.

WHAT AM I PASSIONATE ABOUT? (It can be a dream vacation, a dream job or business, your health, and so forth on.)

_____
_____
_____
_____

HOW DO I DEFINE MY SUCCESS? (Is it people, education, and so forth.)

_____
_____
_____
_____

WHAT IS HOLDING ME BACK? (Myself, lack of money, etc.)

_____
_____
_____
_____

WHAT ARE MY GREATEST ACCOMPLISHMENTS? (Owning a business, Lost 10 lbs, went back to school, etc.)

_____
_____
_____
_____

WHAT WILL I DO TODAY TO GET ONE STEP CLOSER TO MY SUCCESS?

_____
_____
_____
_____

WHAT DO I NEED TO DO TO OVERCOME OBSTACLES AND REACH MY GOALS?

_____
_____
_____
_____

TAKING ACTION: Prime your mind of success and then:

Know what you want.
Take action.
Let your mind of success make course corrections as needed.
Do not stop until you get what you want.

Romans 7:22-25 (NIV) *"22 For in my inner being I delight in God's law; 23 but I see another law at work in me, waging war against the law of my mind and making me a prisoner of the law of sin at work within me. 24 What a wretched man I am! Who will rescue me from this body that is subject to death? 25 Thanks be to God, who delivers me through Jesus Christ our Lord! "*

"So, then, I myself in my mind am a slave to God's law, but in the sinful nature a slave to the law of sin."

    Paul struggled with sin just as we do today. Paul learned what to do when we are over-whelmed by our spiritual battles. We as God's people need to remember that Jesus Christ died for our sins on the cross. You have been set free through His blood and water on the cross from all your sins. Satan knows this, but Satan wants you to believe and think in your mind that you are still sinful.

    We all were born into a sinful nature. We have to learn how to claim and speak freedom to our minds. It was God's son, Jesus Christ, that paid the price for our sins on the cross at Calvary.

It is time for you as God chosen people to feel the Love of Jesus and enjoy the **Victory** through His power. Speak, "Mind! there is no more confusion or doubt…..because through the blood of Jesus Christ I have been set free of all sin. In Jesus name. Amen."

Isaiah 26:3 (NIV) *"You will keep in perfect peace those whose minds is steadfast, because he trusts in you."*

No matter what comes your way, keep your mind on God. Disappointment, setbacks, mistreated, lied on, seasonal jobless, sickness, and so forth on are in the past. Trust that everything is working in your "Favor." I may have been released from one church; but God placed me in another church. God is the guide of your mind. He knows what is best for you; not man. Pray that God remove any and all evil thoughts or emotions towards anyone that have hurt you in the past. You should never ever want to have a judgmental spirit towards God's people. Your mind should continuous stay on the things of God and God's promises for your life. **Decree and declare that you have victory in all your situations everyday.**

Here are some of my personal victories in God: *I have the victory concerning God's marriage to my husband, my children that God has assigned me to, God's businesses, God's strategic plan for the homeless, widows, orphans of this world, and all other kingdom projects that God has not revealed to me.* Today and forever, you will not allow anything to move you out of God's position. You will no longer stumble or waiver in your mind.

"They confronted me in the day of my disaster, but the Lord was my support". (NIV Psalm 18:18)

Isaiah 26:4-7 (KJV) *"4 Trust ye in the Lord for ever; for in the Lord JEHOVAH is everlasting strength: 5 For he bringeth down them that dwell on high; the lofty city, he layeth it low; he layeth it low, even to the ground; he bringeth it even to the dust. 6 The foot shall tread it down, even the feet of the poor, and the steps of the needy. 7 The way of the just is uprightness: thou, most upright, dost weigh the path of the just."*

Stay on the path of righteousness. Righteousness is the state of moral perfection required by God to enter heaven. Righteousness is a requirement. Just as we need certain course requirements to receive a high school diploma; we need righteousness for heaven. Although, we are not perfect, the Bible clearly states that human beings cannot achieve righteousness through their own efforts in Romans 3:20 (NIV) *"Therefore, no one will be declared righteous in his sight by observing the law; rather, through the law we become conscious of sin."*

People receive righteousness through faith in Jesus Christ our Savior. Jesus Christ, the sinless Son of God, took humanity's sin upon Himself and became the willing and perfect sacrifice; and suffered the punishment mankind deserved. God the Father accepted Jesus' sacrifice, through which human beings can become justified. In turn, believers receive righteousness from Christ.

Jesus Christ's perfect righteousness is applied to imperfect humans. Therefore, let us strive at having a perfect and a righteousness mind. I made millions. I was generous to everyone. When I stepped outside of the righteousness of God, I stepped out of the will of God. I was that city that sat high. I praised money and success more than God and my marriage. I was brought down to low, but not to dust. I thank God for His grace and mercy that saved me. Now, I have returned to God's righteousness!

Isaiah 26:10 (KJV) *"Let favour be shewed to the wicked, yet will he not learn righteousness: in the land of uprightness will he deal unjustly, and will not behold the majesty of the Lord.*

Wicked people receive the benefits of God; not blessings. So, let us stop worrying about how this person gets this or have this. I am not saying that all people are wicked. But, you never know how they got to where they are or what it took. Do not be concerned by others wealth; even if they are saved or not saved.

In marriages, the sanctified husband receives the blessings of making millions, while the unsanctified wife receives the benefits; vice verses. The sanctified boss received the blessings of free lunch for all employees once a month. In returned, some unsanctified employees receive the benefits of a free lunch because they are connected to the boss. Even though the unrighteousness receives the benefits, they still don't understand right from wrong.

God's judgment teaches us more than God's gifts (benefits). Stop looking for other people's blessing; because there are only benefits to you. Good gifts fade away, but goodness, righteousness and grace lasts forever in God..... My God! Just think if you are no longer connected to that blessed person, what then? Nothing! I would rather hook up with the blessor; than the benefits of the blessed. I want all of God's blessings; not benefits. Gifts are temporary; but God's blessings are forever.

Jeremiah 17:10 (KJV) *"I the Lord search the heart, I try the reins, even to give every man according to his ways, and according to the fruit of his doings."*

Revelation 2:23 (KJV) *"And I will kill her children with death; and all the churches shall know that I am he which searcheth the reins and hearts: and I will give unto every one of you according to your works."*

Romans 8:27 (KJV) *"And he that searcheth the hearts knoweth what is the mind of the Spirit, because he maketh intercession for the saints according to the will of God."*

Jeremiah 17:9 (KJV) *"The heart is deceitful above all things, and desperately wicked: who can know it?"*

God himself has stated that the heart is deceitful and wicked. Wow! If God says the heart is deceitful and wicked; what is your next step? No, the question is, do you continue to sin and live in deceitfulness and wickedness? How can one not live in deceitfulness and wickedness?

Simple, by reading the Word of God; then your sins will be revealed. Once your sins are revealed, then you can ask God to help you overcome these strongholds called "sin." One thing for sure, we were born in flesh to sin. Psalm 51:5(ESV) *"Behold, I was brought forth in iniquity, and in sin did my mother conceive me"*. The answer to what is your next step? Your next step is to allow God to expose your sins of the flesh through His Word. Galatians 5:19-21 (KJV) *"Now, the works of the flesh are manifest, which are these; Adultery, fornication, uncleanness, lasciviousness, 20 Idolatry, witchcraft, hatred, variance, emulations, wrath, strife, seditions, heresies, 21 Envying, murders, drunkenness, reveling, and such like: of the which I tell you before, as I have also told you in time past, that they which do such things shall not inherit the kingdom of God."*

Once the sins of the flesh have been exposed, then you can confess those sins, repent and ask God for his forgiveness. The exposure of sins of the flesh is on a daily basis; not weekly, monthly or yearly. Don't try to pick one or two of the works of flesh. Choose all of the works of the flesh, because our flesh is composed of all.

This process begins within your mind. Galatians 5:16-18 (KJV) *"This I say then, Walk in the Spirit, and ye shall not fulfill the lust of the flesh: 17 For the flesh lusteth against the Spirit, and the Spirit against the flesh: and these are contrary the one to the other: so that ye cannot do the things that ye would. 18 But if ye be led of the Spirit, ye are not under the law."*

Your mind is the Spirit of God. You have to adjust your mind to godly things. The godly things are the fruit of the spirit. For the fruit of the Spirit is in all goodness, righteousness and truth. You have to desire for righteousness all the day long, everyday. Galatians 5:22-23 (KJV)*"But the fruit of the Spirit is love, joy, peace, longsuffering, gentleness, goodness, faith, 23 Meekness, temperance: against such there is no law."*

Once you have the spiritual mind under God's control, then you can defeat the enemy's thoughts in your mind. Once you have planted the "fruits of the spirit" in your mind, then you can start decreeing and declaring those things that are of God. "**You are Successfully, You are Great, You are an Entrepreneur, You have Victory in your marriage, You have Victory on your job, Your Family is Saved, Your Love Ones are Saved, You are spiritually and financially blessed (pay your tithes and offerings to reap continuous wealth), and so on."**

Matthew 22:37-38 (KJV) *"Jesus said unto him, Thou shalt love the Lord thy God with all thy heart, and with all thy soul, and with all thy mind. 38 This is the first and great commandment."*

Purity of the heart will save the soul. Purity of the heart justifies a Spiritual mind. The heart controls the thinking of mind which saves the soul. Rather than worrying about all we should not do, we should concentrate on all we can do to show our love for God and others.

Deuteronomy 6: 4-5 (KJV) *"4 Hear, O Israel: The Lord our God is one Lord: 5 And thou shalt love the Lord thy God with all thine heart, and with all thy soul, and with all thy might."*

In verse 4, The Lord our God is "One". Israel was entering into a nation where there were many gods. God was warning them beforehand. In today's society, there are many little gods. One of the little gods that God had to destroy for me was the love of money. Other gods could be cars, houses, material things, a man or woman you have deep feelings for, and so forth on. You should love God above all these other gods!

Exercise 8: Set yourself free of the little gods.

Make a list of little **known** gods that needs destroying in your life. Then you can claim victory over them! These little gods are something or someone that you praise everyday; instead of God.

1. Money	6. Internet	11. _____
2. Cars	7. _____	12. _____
3. Houses	8. _____	13. _____
4. Job	9. _____	14. _____
5. Porn	10. _____	15. _____

1 Samuel 15:29 (NIV) *"He who is the Glory of Israel does not lie or change his mind; for he is not a man, that he should change his mind."*

Saul disobeyed the Lord by not killing all the people of the Amalekites and saving some of the plunder for himself. **"The house of Israel does not lie or change his mind."** God wanted Saul to destroy all Amalekites because they were worshippers of idols, sinful and not peaceful. God knew Israelites would not be at peace as long as the Amalekites were around. Although the first execution was not carried out, God still kept his promises to Israel.

Israel had many victories as promised. Israel was given more through David; "eternity of Israel". God gave Israel spiritual strength, victory over their enemies, sin and Satan. Also, Israel was given the world and permanent duration, everlasting salvation, immorality, and eternal life. Just think, you have all of this through God's promises, **"for he is not a man that he should repent."** Because of the strength God gave Israel, they were able to perform whatever he had promised. I had to repent for doubting my husband, marriage and myself. I had to stop allowing circumstances and situations to alter my faith; to make me repent of things that I know I shouldn't say or think. God is unchangeable and never alters his counsel, break his covenant, or reverse his blessings. NO matter how things may seem today, **God Promises are true and your blessings are today!**

No matter what challenges your destiny may bring, God promised success in your marriage, family, job, business, health, and so forth on. You are one of God's vessels to bring people closer to Him. I believe and have faith that my husband and I will ministry to married couples, as well as, single people wanting to marry with God's guidance. *"I decree and declare my family and I will be used for God's kingdom. We will feed the homeless all over the world through God. We will provide shelter and clothing for the needed through God's grace and mercy; and many other projects in Jesus name. Amen."*

You have to speak what you want to do for God's kingdom with a sincere heart; and watch God use you for his purpose, intended for the kingdom.

People come and go in our lives. People are in your life for a season or a reason; to prepare you for the calling of God. There are many people in your circle that can't go where God is trying to elevate you to. This includes: father, mother, brothers, sisters, uncles, aunts, cousins, grandparents, in-laws, friends, and so forth on. This journey is for God.

"1 Peter 2:9 (KJV)....But ye are a chosen generation, a royal priesthood, an holy nation, a peculiar people; that ye should shew forth the praises of him who hath called you out of darkness into his marvelous light:" WE are peculiar people; therefore, we all are children of God! Speak "I am a peculiar person and I am going to withstand the pressure of this evil world with the power of Jesus Christ; and keep moving forward in Jesus Name. Amen."

2 Chronicles 30:12 (NIV) Hezekiah celebrates the Passover.

"Also in Judah the hand of God was on the people to give them unity of mind to carry out what the king and his officials had ordered, following the word of the Lord."

Passover celebration is the yearly reminder of how God delivered the people of Israel. God spared the lives of Israel's firstborn sons in Egypt. The plague would kill the firstborn except those in the homes where the blood of a slain lamb had been painted on the door frames. (Exodus 12:23.) They obeyed and the destroyer passed by these homes. After the plague, Pharaoh freed the Israelites from slavery.

To submit your mind to the Lord means to obey him first; yield your body, mind, will, and emotions to him. By submitting, His Holy Spirit **must guide** and renew every part of you. Anyone that sets their "mind" on the things of God; receives his grace, mercy and forgiveness. Many people from Ephraim, Manasseh, Issachar, and Zulu had not been purified for the feast; but their minds were for God. Hezekiah prayed for forgiveness for them; for the Temple command, because they wanted to obey, even though they were unclean.

After studying this, all I can say is My God! Our obedience brings forth forgiveness, grace and mercy. God will override laws if our "mind" is set on Him. **Forgiveness is for All**, even for lawbreakers; My God! God does not care about laws, (if your "will" is for serving Him), but the "minds" of people. Your mind should be His mind.....

Forget about the criminal charges that may have you thinking that you cannot be successful. Forget about the first marriage that did not succeed; now you know God is in this current marriage and the union will last until death.

Forget about that job that fired you last month, you have a business plan that will take you further; God's business plans!

Psalm 26:2 (NIV)*"Test me, O Lord, and try me, examine my heart and my mind;"*

"God please examine my heart, soul and mind. Clear me of all my sins; seen and unforeseen faults and strongholds of the heart, soul and mind. I trust and thank you God for doing this for me in Jesus name. Amen."

David asked God to do this for him. When I speak these words, I am asking God to test me through trials and tribulations. **"Put me again through the trials and see if I would follow such wicked designs as my enemies impute to me."** David said "See , O God , whether or not I loved murder, and treason, and deceit, I still fear you, Lord ("I fear the Lord")." This plea manifested a most solemn and complete conviction of innocence. This Psalm helps or teaches you that through the divine judgment and the necessity of being in all things profoundly sincere, lest you are found waiting at the last. Your enemies are severe with you; with severity of spite. This brave man, David, this brave woman Eureka, this brave (**put your name**) endures without fear!

I have been tested again of many past sins/wrong doings. There was great testing in my marriage the second time around, but adultery was far from my mind. There came some loneliness and mistreatment, but, I still loved with this loving heart of God. Some family members spoke to me in an ungodly way. I still love them with this loving heart of God. I am to the point now, words can't move me. After they finish with their ungodly words, I will ask "what do you want for dinner???"

My mind is of Jesus Christ and set on the things of God. My Motto is "You are saved, set free and delivered, but its your choice to walk in it." Ephesians 2:8 (KJV) *"For by grace are ye saved through faith; and that not of yourselves: it is the gift of God."* There is nothing on your part to solve. Just live with your heart, soul and mind set on God. Even though my heart has been tested repeatedly, I still say "when God?" I believe, we will have "when God" in our minds on a regular basis. I do believe that everyone has their season. Ecclesiastes 3:1 (NIV) *"There is a time for everything, and a season for every activity under heaven:"* God has a set determined time for when everything shall come into being, how long it shall continue, and in what circumstances. All things have been or shall be were foreordained by God. He has determined the times, before appointed to us for his being, duration and end. Until your time, you just have to stay focus and keep your mind on God; not your circumstances.

Isaiah 26 is a Song of Salvation. Read it, in its entirety. This chapter is of trust, praise and mediation. Parts of the chapters touched my heart based on what I was going through at the time. I read the bible over and over, and over. I realize that each time I read the bible, I get a different revelation. God reveals his secrets to us as we are going through life's trials and seeking his face for the answer. Therefore, it is important to stay in the Word of God as you are going through your trials; especially, the rough ones.

Isaiah 26:3 (NIV) *"You will keep in perfect peace him whose minds is steadfast, because he trusts in you."*

Even though I have had many upsets and disappointments, I feel more connected to God more than ever. I always felt as though I owed someone something. In reality, I only owe myself to God. God sends people your way as a blessing or a lesson. Learn from them. Do not get attached to the people God send to you for that particular season in your life. I have realized that God has put enough godly love in me to spread to many people. I enjoyed the part of my spiritual restoration with some good leaders; but they were in my life for a season to teach me some things; not for friendship; but permanent godly love. The attention that I was seeking needed to come from God; not man. Even though I could not go to my family members in this spiritual season of healing, I could talk to God. God is really guiding and strengthening me everyday of my life. He can do the same for you.

I experienced the " so-called friends" are there as long as you have something to give them. If you can give them money and allow them to know your problems, they are your best friends. When the money is gone, those friends are gone. When they no longer can get into your martial issues or family issues, they are gone. But, God is there all the time waiting and wanting to help.

Romans 1:28-29 (NASB) *"28 And just as they did not see fit to acknowledge God any longer, God gave them over to a depraved mind, to do those things which are not proper, 29 being filled with all unrighteousness, wickedness, greed, evil; full of envy, murder, strife, deceit, malice; they are gossips,"*

The definition of depraved is morally corrupt and wicked. Someone having a depraved mind is a form of murder. The worldly legal definition is an aggravating circumstance of murder in the first degree, where as, the murder involved depravity of mind. Depravity of the mind is a condition characterized by an inherent deficiency of moral sense and integrity. It consists of evil, corrupt and perverted intent which is devoid of regard for human dignity; and which is indifferent to human life. It is a state of mind outrageously horrible or inhuman.

God does not want us to sin. Although, God does not force you to not sin. When you continue to sin, after many attempts to deliver you, God does allow the progression to evil. God is a loving and caring God; if you could just open your heart, mind and soul for him to come in, then you could be more successful.

A depraved mind will cause (1.) People to reject God, (2.) Then people make up their minds and do what they want to do in the flesh, (3.) They grow to hate God, and encourage others to do so. When people continue to reject God, then he allows them to do so. God gives people over to the devil or permits people to experience the natural consequences of sin. Once caught in the downward spiral, no one can pull them out; but (sinners) must trust God all over again and truly believe that Christ died for your sins to put them on the path of escape.

This is what continuously sinning brings to your life……..

Romans 1:26-27(NIV) *"26 Because of this, God gave them over to shameful lusts. Even their women exchanged natural sexual relations for unnatural ones. 27 In the same way the men also abandoned natural relations with women and were inflamed with lust for one another. Men committed shameful acts with other men, and received in themselves the due penalty for their error."*

Sexually sin is the clearest indicator of a society or persons in rebellion against God! …….Woo! God allows us to declare independence from Him. He knows we will become slaves to our own rebellious choice; then we lose our freedom to sin. WE are giving the chose to live in sin or not to live in sin. Jesus died for our freedom not sin; therefore, there is no force to not sin. The Bible is for everyone to read. God knows every creature on this earth. There is no excuse to want to sin once it has been revealed to you. I have learned that the flesh is sinful. I have to stay Fasted and Prayed up. I ask God continuously to keep my mind.

When, I know my mind is set on the fruit of the spirits, then God can control the flesh with his Holy Spirit. But, if you choose to continue to walk in the mind of deceitfulness and wickedness; then God has no control of your mind nor flesh.

I learn that God can't make me obey; but he can teach me to obey. It's a choice to obey. But, once you obey; then God takes control.

Today and everyday, you should not want God to give you over to your sinful flesh! You should want to live through freedom of sin through Jesus Christ. You choose to live in Jesus Christ; not Satan/Sin. Speak, "**My mind, says "no" to sin; but 'yes" to Jesus Christ."**

Romans 8:5-8 (NIV) *"5 Those who live according to the flesh have their minds set on what the flesh desires; but those who live in accordance with the Spirit have their minds set on what the Spirit desires. 6 The mind governed by the flesh is death, but the mind governed by the Spirit is life and peace. 7 The mind governed by the flesh is hostile to God; it does not submit to God's law, nor can it do so. 8 Those who are in the realm of the flesh cannot please God."*

Jesus died on the cross so that our minds are no longer controlled by sinful nature. I have learned how to keep my mouth closed; so I can hear from the Holy Spirit. By doing so, my life has been so peaceful. It is a time to speak and not to speak. I am in a season of my life that I am not speaking much; but allowing God to control my mind, thoughts and actions. I had some hostile intention deep down inside of me at one point of my life. God delivered me and set me free from hostility.

By me not being so hostile, because of my circumstances, allowed our God to be in control of my destiny.

My God! Revelation! The Holy Spirit reigns in a godly mind; not a hostile mind. I never again want to be hostile or anger to others because of my circumstances or situation. Hostility means a sinful mind. A sinful mind cannot be successful in life. Satan wants to hold our minds hostage; but Jesus Christ has broken that curse/bond over our minds when He died on the cross as man (human) for our sinful nature, then rose again in Spirit. Adam listened to a god (snake) and brought sin on everyone (Genesis 3:1-20). Jesus died for that sin. Now, allow God to control your heart, soul and mind; not man, flesh, Satan or other gods.

Romans 12:2 (NIV) *"Do not conform to the pattern of this world, but be transformed by the renewing of your mind. Then you will be able to test and approve what God's will is—his good, pleasing and perfect will."*

Our mind is not of this world. You really can have a godly mind living in a sinful world. Sin is always going to be here until Jesus Christ return. Temptation is always a way of Satan to win you over to him. Romans 8:36 (NIV) *"As it is written: "For your sake we face death all day long; we are considered as sheep to be slaughtered."* We have to die to our flesh daily; and daily renew our minds of the fruit of the spirit; tested and approved to receive the godly mind that is good, pleasing and in perfect will. Once your mind is set on the things of God, **daily**, then you can live in success, peace and joy.

Romans 14:13 (NIV) *"Therefore let us stop passing judgment on one another. Instead, make up your mind not to put any stumbling block or obstacle in your brother's way."*

Be strong in faith, but sensitive to others. Find some type of ministry to serve in that will keep your mind focused. During my season of not operating a business, I caters my time to being sensitive to others. I volunteer at Helping Hands Depot, Inc (Jacksonville, Florida). I help feed the homeless at the Jacksonville Florida Landing. I visited the nursing home. I walk the streets of Jacksonville, Florida; just to pray in the atmosphere. This helps me to understand God's passion for all of mankind. Do not be too holy that you miss out on loving and caring for others; the way Jesus Christ did for us on the cross. Because we don't consume alcohol, smoke or entertain any other ungodly actions, doesn't mean that we are better than anyone else or have permission criticize them.

You have to recognize your strongholds in order to be delivered and set free. Strongholds are walls or fortresses around beliefs and emotions to protect us from further pain. An important part of healing and transforming the deep wounds of life requires divinely pulling down the strongholds that are used to take away the pain, temporarily. During my season of pain, consuming alcohol became my stronghold. I dealt with the consumption of alcohol when I stepped out of my marriage. Therefore, I am no better than anyone struggling with the stronghold of alcohol or any other stronghold. I found Jesus Christ. I let go of my strongholds; and I choose not to let go of God. Instead, just pray for the ones that are still struggling with strongholds.

Ask God to deliver them of their strongholds. Everyone has been delivered from something: partying, adultery, cursing, and so forth on. Find a ministry that you can help and serve others. Matthew 20:28 (NLT) *"For even the Son of Man came not to be served but to serve others and to give his life as a ransom for many."* Jesus Christ was a servant to us. Why are you not serving others???

I will use the consumption of alcohol as one of my strongholds for my immediate and extended family. I realized that alcohol has consumed some our **Great leaders** that have been called for God's kingdom. I pray hard for anyone that consumes alcohol; and other strongholds. I battled with the consumption of alcohol and some of my close family members and friends are battling with the same stronghold. I have learned not to nag them of this stronghold; but to use the Holy Spirit to speak to them through my silence. You know you can stand by someone and pray in your mind for their healing and deliverance. (But, do not use the silence as a form of control; that is a form of witchcraft.) When I learned this, the devil had to watch out! I do this more than calling people out and asking them if they need prayer. By me praying in silence allows me to be mindful of a person's maturity in God. It's our actions/lifestyle; not voice, that brings people to God. My God! **Love everyone until the healing and deliverance has taken place!**

2 Corinthians 10:4 (KJV) *"(For the weapons of our warfare are not carnal, but mighty through God to the pulling down of strong holds.)"*

In John 8:31-36, Jesus tells us that we can be held in bondage due to strongholds in our lives. And His solution was to, *"continue in my word... and ye shall know the truth, and the truth shall make you free"* (NASB v.31- 32).

Strongholds are torn down as we meditate on God's Word, which is truth!

Exercise 9: Tearing Down of Strongholds.

List your known strongholds and begin tearing them down in Jesus Christ name. Amen:

Strongholds are high levels of demonic influence (not possession) in any area(s) of the spiritual faculties of an individual. The spiritual faculties consist of your mind, your emotions and your will power. Some examples of sinful behaviors are: atheism, unbelief, stealing, greed, alcohol addiction, drugs, sexual sins, promiscuity, pornography, homosexuality, uncontrollable anger (temper tantrums), compulsive gambling, and so on are considered as strongholds in one's life. The feeling is easily pulled to or controlled by whatever matter that is entrenched into your lifestyle.

_____
_____

EUREKA BUTLER

Chapter Five

Division in the Church

Division in the Church

1 Corinthians 1:10 (ESV) *"I appeal to you, brothers, by the name of our Lord Jesus Christ, that all of you agree, and that there be no divisions among you, but that you be united in the same mind and the same judgment."*

Focus more and more on Jesus Christ, our Lord, and his purpose for dying on the cross for our life. Stop focusing on what is around you. Distractions of this world come to make you lose focus. **We all have a successful life that is of God and from God.** You need to identify the success and work; united in mind and thought with God. Your success is to give back to God; for his kingdom purpose. God's kingdom is your family, church and community. People make up the family, church and community. Therefore, **WE are the family, We are the church and WE are the community!**

1 Corinthians 14:14 *"14 For if I pray in a tongue, my spirit prays, but my understanding is unfruitful. 15 What is the conclusion then? I will pray with the spirit, and I will also pray with the understanding. I will*

sing with the spirit, and I will also sing with the understanding. (NKJV)."

The mind is thinking, reasoning and judgmental. In our mind, we need to understand, have knowledge and revelation of what we are praying and singing. Through reading the Word of God, I have gotten much revelation to many scriptures, prayers, songs, and prophecy. Revelation and understanding is what God gives to you; if you would mediate and study his Word for success.

Romans 16:17-20 (NIV) *"17 I urge you, brothers and sisters, to watch out for those who cause divisions and put obstacles in your way that are contrary to the teaching you have learned. Keep away from them. 18 For such people are not serving our Lord Christ, but their own appetites. By smooth talk and flattery they deceive the minds of naive people. 19 Everyone has heard about your obedience, so I rejoice because of you; but I want you to be wise about what is good, and innocent about what is evil.*

20 The God of peace will soon crush Satan under your feet. The grace of our Lord Jesus be with you."

As I mention before, I use to listen to the scriptures of God from the pastor and songs from the choir just to be informed. Now, God has given me much revelation of the scriptures. When, I started paying close attention to gospel music, I realize the songs should come from scriptures. That's why we need to be careful of what we listen to. Not every word from a leader or person of God is of God. Our mind need to be saturate with the Word of God; so that we will know for ourselves how to be successful in life. There are so many lost people in this world because they are not getting their confirmation from the bible, but from man.

Here a few scriptures that helped me along the way to a successful mind.

1. I was told to keep my mouth closed in a disagreement with my family. Why?

Proverbs 15:1-2 (NIV) *"A gentle answer turns away wrath, but a harsh word stirs up anger. 2 The tongue of the wise adorns knowledge, but the mouth of the fool gushes, folly."*

2. I should get up early in the morning to pray and cook for my family. Why?

Proverbs 31:10-31 (KJV)

10 Who can find a virtuous woman? for her price is far above rubies.
11 The heart of her husband doth safely trust in her, so that he shall have no need of spoil.
12 She will do him good and not evil all the days of her life.
13 She seeketh wool, and flax, and worketh willingly with her hands.
14 She is like the merchants' ships; she bringeth her food from afar.
15 She riseth also while it is yet night, and giveth meat to her household, and a portion to her maidens.
16 She considereth a field, and buyeth it: with the fruit of her hands she planteth a vineyard.
17 She girdeth her loins with strength, and strengtheneth her arms.
18 She perceiveth that her merchandise is good: her candle goeth not

out by night.
19 She layeth her hands to the spindle, and her hands hold the distaff.
20 She stretcheth out her hand to the poor; yea, she reacheth forth her hands to the needy.
21 She is not afraid of the snow for her household: for all her household are clothed with scarlet.
22 She maketh herself coverings of tapestry; her clothing is silk and purple.
23 Her husband is known in the gates, when he sitteth among the elders of the land.
24 She maketh fine linen, and selleth it; and delivereth girdles unto the merchant.
25 Strength and honour are her clothing; and she shall rejoice in time to come.
26 She openeth her mouth with wisdom; and in her tongue is the law of kindness.
27 She looketh well to the ways of her household, and eateth not the bread of idleness.
28 Her children arise up, and call her blessed; her husband also, and he praiseth her.
29 Many daughters have done virtuously, but thou excellest them all.
30 Favour is deceitful, and beauty is vain: but a woman that feareth the Lord, she shall be praised.
31 Give her of the fruit of her hands; and let her own works praise her in the gates.

3. Why not argue back with family members that does not understand my purpose?

2 Timothy 2:23 (NIV) *"Don't have anything to do with foolish and stupid arguments, because you know they produce quarrels."*

2 Timothy 2:14 (NIV) *"Keep reminding God's people of these things. Warn them before God against quarreling about words; it is of no value, and only ruins those who listen."*

4. Why I should not harbor pain, which was put on me by others?

Psalm 55:21-23. *"21 His speech was smoother than butter, But his heart was war; His words were softer than oil, Yet they were drawn swords. 22 Cast your burden upon the LORD and He will sustain you; He will never allow the righteous to be shaken. 23 But You, O God, will bring them down to the pit of destruction; Men of bloodshed and deceit will not live out half their days. But, I will trust in You." (NASB)*

1 Peter 5:6-8 *"6 Therefore humble yourselves under the mighty hand of God, that He may exalt you at the proper time, 7 casting all your anxiety on Him, because He cares for you. 8 Be of sober spirit, be on the alert. Your adversary, the devil, prowls around like a roaring lion, seeking someone to devour." (NASB)*

5. Why should I pray for my enemies? I had a lot of people to come against me concerning some legal issues. Why should I pray for them?

Matthew 5:44 (KJV) *"But I say unto you, Love your enemies, bless them that curse you, do good to them that hate you, and pray for them which despitefully use you, and persecute you;"*

6. No one assisted me in paying for my bills when the business closed. Why nobody was there for me financially? Somebody was; it was God!

Psalm 121:1-8 (NIV) A song of ascents.

*1 I lift up my eyes to the mountains—
where does my help come from?
2 My help comes from the Lord,
the Maker of heaven and earth.
3 He will not let your foot slip—
he who watches over you will not slumber;
4 indeed, he who watches over Israel
will neither slumber nor sleep.
5 The Lord watches over you—
the Lord is your shade at your right hand;
6 the sun will not harm you by day,
nor the moon by night.
7 The Lord will keep you from all harm—
he will watch over your life;
8 the Lord will watch over your coming and going
both now and forevermore.*

2 Corinthians 13:11 (NIV) *"11 Finally, brothers and sisters, rejoice! Strive for full restoration, encourage one another, be of one mind, live in peace. And the God of love and peace will be with you."*

Paul and the Corinthians had many problems and difficulties in the church. Paul is saying that we will have the same issues as they had; neglect, denial, withdrawals, or bitterness. But, you must apply the principles of God's Word and just not hear it on Sunday; but live it in your everyday lives. You need to hear the Word of God daily and mediate on the Word daily through reading and studying the Bible.

By now, you should have in your mind that you want to aim for perfection, you want to listen to His appeals, be of one mind, and live in peace. WE must be on "**one accord**" with the things of God. The way you can test your "**Faith** "of unity is 2 Corinthians 13:5 (NIV) *"5 Examine yourselves to see whether you are in the faith; test yourselves. Do you not realize that Christ Jesus is in you—unless, of course, you fail the test?* " The results of the testing are growing awareness of Christ; it's the presence and power of Christ in our lives. It is the loving, caring and encouraging one another. Lifting, one another in **Hope**. Also, in 2 Corinthians 6:6(NIV) *"in purity, understanding, patience and kindness; in the Holy Spirit and in sincere love;"*

Philippians 3:19 (NIV) *"Their destiny is destruction, their god is their stomach, and their glory is in their shame. Their mind is on earthly things."*

Paul says that people cater to their appetites; not to the things of God, but of earthly things. Earthly things are work, job, money, houses, cars, relationships, circumstances/relationships, and the lack of. Your mind should be on praying, fasting, worshipping God, loving and caring for others, repenting, confessing, and encouraging one another.

When the family business closed, I felt like a failure. I helped many people during their growing season of success. In return, after the business closed, people were trying to see what they can take from me. For example, my house furniture, office furniture, office equipment, and so forth on. They actually believed that I wouldn't escalate in success again. Yes, I made millions. I lived a lavish lifestyle with the millions; but when I stepped out of my marriage and the will of God, those millions disappeared, rapidly. I was spending out of control. I was so busy focusing on the success from God, that I forgot to maintain a relationship with God. My past business mistakes brought a lot of hurt and pain.

But, I began to read the bible more and more to received a better understanding of God, family, church and business. In spite of my disappointments, God still kept my mind, because I sought after the things of God, hastily. This time around I have gain much spiritual wealth that has given me the stability, peace, love, and a caring spirit that is needed to run this race for God. There is nothing like a peace of mind. Now, I have forgotten what is behind me, and pressing towards the "Greater." My mind is set on the "Prize" for which God has called me; heavenward in Christ Jesus.

Notes:

What race are you running?_____

Whose prize are you seeking?_____

"HEY " GOD........I   CHOOSE   TO   BE   SUCCESSFUL!

Chapter Six

Pressing Toward the Goal

Philippians 3:12-16 (NKJV) *"12 Not that I have already attained or am already perfected; but I press on, that I may lay hold of that for which Christ Jesus has also laid hold of me. 13 Brethren, I do not count myself to have apprehended; but one thing I do, forgetting those things which are behind and reaching forward to those things which are ahead, 14 I press toward the goal for the prize of the upward call of God in Christ Jesus. 15 Therefore let us, as many as are mature, have this mind; and if in anything you think otherwise, God will reveal even this to you. 16 Nevertheless, to the degree that we have already attained, let us walk by the same rule, let us be of the same mind."*

God has called Eureka for **"Greatness."** God has called **(you name)** for "**Greatness**." With a purpose, all that I have attained so far through the Word of God, I will use it to help others to never give up on their dreams , goals, or plans? I want the nation to know that after you turn to God for his guidance, whatever else is needed, God will make clear for you and I.

Colossians 2:18 (NIV) *"Do not let anyone who delights in false humility and the worship of angels disqualify you. Such a person also goes into great detail about what they have seen; they are puffed up with idle notions by their unspiritual mind."*

Unspiritual mind means that one is not connected to God; or that one has no knowledge of His son Jesus Christ. WE should have a "**Christ-like mind.**" God allows people in your life for a blessing or a lesson. Many people will try to compare your success with their success. They will try to convince you that their way is the best way. You say "**But God**!"

Colossians 2:16-19 (NKJV) 16 *"6 So let no one judge you in food or in drink or regarding a festival or a new moon or sabbaths, 17 which are a shadow of things to come, but the substance is of Christ. 18 Let no one cheat you of your reward, taking delight in false humility and worship of angels, intruding into those things which he has not seen, vainly puffed up by his fleshly mind, 19 and not holding fast to the Head, from whom all the body, nourished and knit together by joints and ligaments, grows with the increase that is from God.."*

The bible is a guide; not people beliefs. If you do not understand something or get confused or frustrated with something that someone has said to you, ask for a scripture to back up what they are saying. By doing this, will keep a lot of people from talking in your ear.

1 John 4:1-2 (NKJV) *" 1 Beloved, do not believe every spirit, but test the spirits, whether they are of God; because many false prophets have gone out into the world. 2 By this you know the Spirit of God: Every spirit that confesses that Jesus Christ has come in the flesh is of God,"*

Technology is a quick reference. Use your phone to type in what they are saying and see if a scripture backs their statement. I use Google all the time on the spot to clarify someone's statement concerning the Word of God. I will never be lost again about the things of God. The Internet can have mistakes, but it can be that source for that moment, until you can get to a Bible for further clarifications. Even when I am witnessing to people, I use the Internet as a quick reference guide.

Our mind should be set on God's Word. Get your mind filled with the Word of God so the Holy Spirit can lead and guide you into all the promises of God.

1 Thessalonians 4:11-12 (NKJV) *"11 that you also aspire to lead a quiet life, to mind your own business, and to work with your own hands, as we commanded you, 12 that you may walk properly toward those who are outside, and that you may lack nothing."*

My God! Do not depend on others! God has given you *"your*

Blessed hands" to work for His kingdom. Speak, **"God, I thank you for blessing my hands for Kingdom success! God, I thank you for controlling my mind and my destiny. My success is in you, God. God teach me to do your will with the hands you have given me, in Jesus name. Amen."**

"Mind is the self as deeply contemplating."

"Heart is the self manifesting a complex of attitudes."

"Will is self as choosing and deciding."

"Spirit is the self when thought of apart from earth by connection."

"HEY " GOD........I CHOOSE TO BE SUCCESSFUL!

Chapter Seven

The Strength of Success

To bear the yoke means to willingly come under God's discipline and learn what he wants to teach you concerning success. The way to get Gods attention is:

1. Silent reflection on what God wants.

2. Repent humility.

3. Self control in the face of adversity.

4. Confidence and patience.

5. Depend on the divine Teacher to bring about loving lessons in our

lives for success.

In Deuteronomy 6:5(NIV)*"Love the Lord your God with all your heart and with all your soul and with all your strength"* and Matthew 22: 37-39 *"…………..Love the Lord your God with all your heart and with all your soul and with your mind…………"*

I believe in the Old Testament, God knew that it would take **strength** in order to obey the commands of God. Once the Israelites were delivered out of Egypt and crossed the Jordan River to the Promised Land, God knew it would take some **strength** for the people of Israel to abide and keep the commandment of God. In the New Testament, Jesus Christ died on the cross for our sins and strength. Jesus Christ is our strength to endure the pain and sufferings that life brings us. Instead of you worrying about all you should not do, you should be concentrating on all you can do to show your love for God and others; because Jesus is doing the Work.

What is strength? Strength is Power, Might, Will, and it is Strong. Strength is what needed to help you to be successful. We may know the Word of God, but it takes the strength of God to stay with your husband or wife when one spouse has committed adultery. It takes the strength of the Lord to reestablish and rebuild a business, after one business failed. It takes the strength of the Lord to continue to praise God, when the doctor gives you some negative news about your health. It takes the strength of the Lord to keep pressing on, when you have gone on 10 job interviews and no one has called you back, yet. It takes the strength of the Lord to continue encouraging other children, when your child is facing ten years in prison. Life

brings about plenty of challenges, but it is the strength of the Lord that keeps us in "the perfect peace of God."

Exodus 15: 2 (NIV) *"The Lord is my strength and my song; he has become my salvation. He is my God, and I will praise him, my father's God, and I will exalt him."*

Exodus 15 is a song of Moses and Miriam. Moses song of deliverance and praise after God led Israel out of Egypt and saved them by departing the Red Sea. Also, Miriam joined in the singing. When you are pressing your way to success, find a song to lift your heart and the heart of others. Exodus 15 was a song celebrating God's victory, lifting the hearts and voices of people outward and upward. After God gives you the success that you been "longing fulfilled", give Him a joy-filled song back to "thank Him ." Psalms and hymns can be a great way of expressing relief. A song gives praises and thanks after a troubled storm in your life. Singing godly filled songs will bring rest to the soul. All your burdens will be lifted and you will find the strength that was hidden behind your burdens. My little hymn in this season of my life is "Lord I thank You, Lord I Adore you, Lord I thank, Lord I Adore you........."

Judges 15:18-19 (NIV) *"Because he was very thirsty, he cried out to the Lord, "You have given your servant this great victory. Must I now die of thirst and fall into the hands of the uncircumcised?" 19 Then God opened up the hollow place in Lehi, and water came out of it. When Samson drank, his strength returned and he revived. So the spring was called En Hakkore, and it is still there in Lehi."*

Samson became very weak physically and emotionally during the battle. After a great victory, he slipped into a self-pity state of mind, "Must I now die of thirst". In your journey to success, you may become weak. Nevertheless, God is still in control. You have to realize the victory is not yours; it is the Lords! Samson had gotten very vulnerable and he thought God owed him something. God's strength gave Samson victory from the beginning to the end. Every trial that you overcome, remember it is God that gives you strength to endure from the beginning to the end. During your times of success, avoid temptations to assume God owes you for your efforts. It was God, which equipped you for the task in the beginning. Remember severe depression often follows great achievements, so don't be surprised if you feel drained after a personal victory. In the end, God opened up the hollow place in Lehi and water came out of it. Therefore, God will renew your strength after a victorious battle and pour out His blessings, in his timing.

Read and Study the story of Samson in Judges 13-16.

It is sad to be remembered for what one might have been. Samson had tremendous potential. Not many people started life with credentials like Samson. Born as a result of God's plan, in the loves of Manoah and his wife; Samson was to do a great work for God. Samson was anointed to deliver Israel out of the hands of the Philistines. God gave Samson enormous physical strength to accomplish this task.

Samson wasted his strength on practical jokes and getting out of brawls. Also, Samson wasted his strength to satisfy women he loved.

We may see him as a failure for these actions; but, not through God's eyes. There may be many of us, which have given up on our goals and dreams, for someone or something. The story of Samson will give you the encouragement you need; it is never too late to be successful. Samson was known as the judge in Israel, who spent his last days in the enemy prison. Yes, Samson wasted his life. He could have strengthened his nation. He could have returned his people to the worship of God. He could have wiped out the Philistines. However, even though he did none of those things, Samuel still accomplished the purpose announced by the angel who visited his parents before his birth (Judges). **In his final act, Samson <u>began to rescue</u> Israel from the Philistines.**

The New Testament does not mention Samson's failures or his heroic feats of strength. Hebrews 11:33, Samson is listed with the others "who through faith conquered kingdoms, administered justice, and gained what was promised;" and in other ways were given superhuman aid. God turned his failures and defeats into victory. Samson's story teaches us that it is never to late to start over. It does not matter how badly we have failed in the past. Today is not too late for you to put your complete trust in God. All the setbacks, disappointments, anger, resentment, despair, worthlessness, hopelessness, fearfulness, vengeance, and self-pity are behind you. Today, put all your trust in God; so He can complete in you what He has plan for your life for His kingdom purpose.

II Samuel 22:33 (NIV) *"Its is God who arms me with strength and makes my way perfect."*

David says "the Lord is our Rock, Fortress, Deliverer, Refuge, Shield, Horn of Salvation, Stronghold, Savior, and Lamp. God is our everything. God is Saving, Worthy of Praise, Hearing, Angry (against enemies), Rescuing, Rewarding, Seeing, Faithful, Showing (revealing) himself, Shrewd, Powerful, Strong, Perfect, Pure, Flawless, Shielding (us from enemies), Giving, Gentle, Preserving, and Living (on the inside of us)." Everyday repeat these words to your soul until you feel something breaking on the inside of you. God wants you to be broken; so he can complete you.

I can remember I received a phone call from someone back home in Quincy, Florida. In the conversation, this person started repeating all these negative words about me concerning my health; supposedly what people were saying about me. God had me looking so different and vibrant, until my enemies were so confused, when I went back for the first time, in a long time. Based on all the negativity, I can truly say that **"God's gift looks good on me."** Immediately I started speaking blessings over my curses and cursors. Because I feel the "Joy", that David feels. I am filled with **"Joy of the Lord."** I had to realize that it's my enemies that are keeping the Lord's strength, so strong within me; not the so-called friends. As long as I have enemies, the more I need to ask God to strengthen me to endure. The more enemies, the more I pray this words, " God **do not let me be put to shame in front of my enemies.**" Thus, this far and forever more, I have never been put to shame in front of my enemies, because of my past.

Psalm (NIV) 25:1-3 *"1 To you, O Lord, I lift up my soul; 2 in you I trust, O my God. Do not let me be put to shame, nor let my enemies triumph over me. 3 No one whose hope is in you will ever be put to shame, but they will be put to shame who are treacherous without excuse."*

Now, I say. The more people talk about you, the more you should pray for Your(God) strength to love them. Then, people will see your "Joy", in spite of, and turn to your God for strength for their Joy! …….My God!

Psalm 23:5-6 (NIV) *"You prepare a table before me in the presence of my enemies. You anoint my head with oil; my cup overflows 6 Surely goodness and love will follow me all the days of my life, and I will dwell in the house of the Lord forever."*

1 Chronicles 16:11(NIV) *"Look to the Lord and his strength; seek his face always."*

1 Chronicle 16 is David "**Psalms of thanks**." Praise and thanksgiving should be a regular part of your routine; not just for a celebration or when God has given you victory over something. When we praise God continuously, you will never take any of God's blessings or success for granted. Look for the Lord's strength in your marriage, for your health, for parenting, on the job, in the community, and in your business. God's strength will carry you farther than you can imagine; just seek His face.

1 Chronicles 29:12 (NIV) *"Wealth and honor come from you; you are the ruler of all things. In your hands are strength and power to exalt and give strength to all."*

Nothing that is good and perfect lasts unless it is rooted in God's unchanging character. God is the ruler of all things. It is God's hand that give us the strength and power to gain his wealth and honor.

Nothing belongs to you and I. God controls the wealth and honor; not man. Stop giving praises to your boss that gave you the promotion; give praises to God for allowing you to receive the promotion. Stop giving praises to yourself for winning a contract bid from the City; give praises to God for allowing you to win the contract bid from the City. (1 Chronicles 29:10-13)

Nehemiah 8:10 (NIV) *"Nehemiah said, "Go and enjoy choice food and sweet drinks, and send some to those who have nothing prepared. This day is sacred to our Lord. Do not grieve, for the joy of the Lord is your strength."*

Nehemiah was a layman; not a member of the religious establishment or a prophet. He was motivated by his relationship with God. Such people are crucial to God's work in all aspects of life. No matter what your work or role in life, view it as God's special calling to serve him. God can accomplish his purposes through you, beginning right where you are. *You may be a waitress at a local restaurant. You may be a janitor working in the late night hours. You may be a cashier at the local grocery store. You may have been abused when you were a child.* **God has a purpose for you...**

The people in Jerusalem wept openly when they heard God's law and realized how far they were from obeying them. No matter your position, your situation, or circumstances; you are never too far from obeying God. Actually, you are closer than you think you are. Just confess your sins and repent; and God will immediately forgive you of your sins. But Ezra told them they should be filled with " **joy**" because the day was "**holy**." It was time to celebrate and give gifts to those in need. A *Celebration* is not to be self-centered. Therefore, *Success* is not to be self-centered. This celebration gave those in need an opportunity to celebrate, as well. Often when we celebrate and give to others (even when we do not feel like it), we are strengthened "**spiritually**" and filled with "**Joy**." Enter into a celebration that honors God and allow him to fill you with "Joy. "

Practice a habit of giving ....without receiving anything back.

1. Give your time by babysitting for a single mom without pay.

2.

3.

4.

5.

6.

7.

8.

"HEY" GOD.....I CHOOSE TO BE SUCCESSFUL!

Chapter Eight

Fasting and Praying

I believe in the power of fasting and praying. Fasting and praying are the equivalent of a spiritual atomic bomb that our Lord has given us to destroy the strongholds of evil and to usher us into a spiritual harvest around the world. We must use the power of one of the most potent weapons that we have: Prayer and Fasting. Jesus declared that some things could only be removed by prayer and fasting (Matthew 9:29). In order for you to be effective in your fasting, you must prepare. It is better to be successful for a short time then to set goals that you cannot fulfill. Fasting is a lifestyle for me. I do not have to wait until the pastor calls a church fast. I fast because I know and understand the power of Praying and Fasting.

The extent to which you are able to dedicate yourself to receiving all God has for you will depend on several things:

1. Your willingness to abandon your personal will to God's will.

2. The physical condition of your body. Some people believe that their medical conditions will not allow for fasting. No matter what your condition is, you can fast! The question is, how?

3. The extent that you prepare yourself to undertake the tasks.

Step 1: Set your Objective.

The purpose for fasting. Is it for spiritual renewal, guidance, for healing, for the resolution of problems, for special grace to handle a difficult situation???? Ask the Holy Spirit to clarify His objectives for your prayer fast.

2 Chronicles 7:14 (NKJV)*"if my people, who are called by my name, will humble themselves and pray and seek my face and turn from their wicked ways, then I will hear from heaven and will forgive their sin and will heal their land."*

Step 2: Make your commitment.

Pray about the kind of fast you should undertake. Jesus implied that all His followers should fast. (Matthew 6:6-18)

a. How long will you fast? one meal, two meals, one day, a week, several weeks, forty days (beginners should start slowly, building up to longer fasts.)

b. The type of fast God wants you to undertake (such as water only, or water and juices; what kind of juices you will drink and how often.)

c. What physical or social activities you will restrict?

d. How much time each day you will devote to prayer and God's Word?

Making these commitments ahead of time will help you sustain your fast when physical temptations and life's pressures tempt you to abandon it.

Step 3: Prepare Yourself Spiritually.

The foundation of fasting and praying is repentance. Un-confessed sin will hinder your prayers. Here are several things you can do to prepare your heart:

a. Ask God to help you make a comprehensive list of your sins.

b. Confess every sin that the Holy Spirit calls to your remembrance and accept God's forgiveness

(I John 1:9 NIV) If we confess our sins, he is faithful and just and will forgive us our sins and purify us from all unrighteousness.

c. Seek forgiveness from all whom you have offended, and forgive all who have hurt you (Mark 11:25; Luke 11:4; 17:3, 4)

d. Make restitution as the Holy Spirit leads you.

e. Ask God to fill you with Holy Spirit according to His command in (Ephesians 5:18) and His promise in (1 John 5:14, 15).

f. Surrender your life fully to Jesus Christ as your Lord and Master- refuse to obey your worldly nature (Romans 12:1, 2)

g. Meditate on the attribute of God, His love, sovereignty, power, wisdom, faithfulness, grace, compassion, and others (Psalms 48:9, 10; 103:1-8, 11-13)

h. Begin your time of fasting and prayer with an expectant heart (Hebrew 11:6).

i. Praise and give thanks to God continually in all ways on all days, regardless of your circumstances.

j. Love God with all your heat, soul, and mind (Matthew 22:37)

k. Read, study, mediate on, and memorize God's holy, inspired, inerrant Word daily

(Colossians 3:16).

l. Pray without ceasing (1 Thessalonians 5:17).

Step 4: Prepare Yourself Physically.

Fasting requires reasonable precautions. Consult God before taking yourself off any medications. Physical preparation makes the drastic change in your eating routine a little easier so that you can turn your full attention to the Lord in prayer.

a. Do not rush into your fast.

b. Prepare your body. Eat smaller meals before starting a fast. Avoid high-fat and sugary foods.

c. If you are on medication, slowly take yourself off the medication until you are spiritually connected to God to remove yourself completely off your medications.

Fasting & Praying

Your time of fasting and prayer has come. You are abstaining from all solid foods and have begun to seek the Lord. Here are some helpful suggestions to consider:

a. Avoid drugs, even natural herbal drugs and homeopathic remedies

b. Limit your activity.

c. Exercise only moderately. Walk each day if convenient and comfortable.

d. Rest as much as your schedule will permit.

e. Prepare yourself for temporary personality changes, such as impatience, crankiness, and anxiety.

f. Expect some physical discomforts, especially on the second day. You may have fleeting hunger pains, dizziness. Withdrawals from caffeine and sugar may cause headaches. Physical annoyances may also include weakness, tiredness, or sleeplessness. The first two or three days are usually the hardest. As you continue to fast, you will likely experience a sense of well-being both physically and spiritually. However, should you feel hunger pains, increase your liquid in-take.

Step 5: Put Yourself on a Schedule.

For maximum spiritual benefit, set aside ample time to be alone with the Lord. Listen for His leading. The more time you spend with Him, the more meaningful your fast will be.

During mealtime, replace the meal with prayer!

Morning

-Begin your day in praise and worship.

-Read and meditate on God's Word, preferably on your knees.

-Invite the Holy Spirit to work in you, to do His will and do His good pleasure according to

    Philippians 2:13.

-Invite God to use you. Ask Him to show you his will for you in you life; how to influence your world, your family, your church, your community, your country, and beyond.

-Pray for His vision for your life and empowerment to do His will.

Noon

-Return to prayer and God's Word.

-Take a short prayer walk.

-Spend time in intercessory prayer for your community's and leaders, for the worlds un-reached millions, and for your family or special needs.

Evening

-Get alone for an unhurried time, of "seeking His face."

-If others are fasting with you, meet together for prayer.

-Avoid television, radio, ipods, the internet or any other distraction that may dampen your spiritual focus.

Step 6: End of Fast Gradually.

When your designated time for fasting is finished, you will begin to eat again. But, how you break your fast is extremely important for you physical and spiritual well-being. Begin eating gradually. Do not eat solid foods immediately after you fast. Suddenly reintroducing solid food to your stomach and digestive tract will likely have negative, even dangerous, consequences. Try several smaller meals or snacks each day.

Gradually return to regular eating with several small snacks during the first few days. Start with a little soup and fresh fruit such as watermelon and cantaloupe. Advance to a few tablespoons of solid foods such as raw fruits and vegetables or a raw salad and baked potato.

Step 7: Expect Results.

If you sincerely humble yourself before the Lord, repent, pray, and seek God's face. If you consistently meditate on His Word, you will experience a heightened awareness of His presence (John 14:21). The Lord will give you fresh, new spiritual insights. Your confidence and faith in God, will be strengthened. You will feel mentally, spiritually, and physically refreshed. You will see answers to your prayers. A single fast, however, is not a spiritual cure all. Just as we need fresh infillings of the Holy Spirit daily, we also need new times of fasting before God. A 24-hour fast each week has been greatly rewarding to, many Christians.

It takes time to build your spiritual fasting muscles. If you fall to make it through your first fast, do not be discouraged. You may have tried to fast too long the first time out, or you may need to strengthen your understanding and resolve. As soon as possible, undertake another fast until you do succeed. God will honor you for your faithfulness.

Different Types of Fast:

Full Fast

Drink only liquids (you establish the number of days).

The Daniel Fast

Eat no meat, no sweets and no bread. Drink water and juice. Eat fruits and vegetables.

3-Day Fast

This fast can be a Full Fast, Daniel Fast or give up at least one item of food.

Partial Fast

A partial fast is from 6:00 am to 3:00 pm or from sun up to sundown. You can select from three types of fasting —a Full Fast, Daniel Fast or give up at least one item of food.

Scripture References for Fasting:

Matthew 6:16-18, Matthew 9:14-15, Luke 18:9-14

Relation to Prayer and Reading of the Word:

1 Samuel 1:6-8, 17-18, Nehemiah 1:4, Daniel 9:3, 20, Joel 2:12, Luke 2:37, Acts 10:30, Acts 13:2

Corporate Fasting:

1 Samuel 7:5-6, Ezra 8:21-23, Nehemiah 9:1-3, Joel 2:15-16, Jonah 3:5-10, Acts 27:33-37

Remember, it is the attitude of a heart sincerely seeking Him to which God responds with a blessing (Isaiah 58, Jeremiah 14:12, 1 Corinthians 8:8). May God greatly bless you, as you fast!

Neglecting God and others by…..

Sexual immorality (Galatians 5:19)

Impurity (Galatians 5:19)

Lust (Colossians 3:5)

Hatred (Galatians 5:20)

Discord (Galatians 5:20)

Jealousy (Galatians 5:20)

Anger (Galatians 5:20)

Selfish ambition (Galatians 5:20)

Dissension (Galatians 5:20)

Arrogance (2 Corinthians 12:20)

Envy (Galatians 5:21)

Murder (Revelation 22:12-16)

Idolatry (Galatians 5:20; Ephesians 5:5)

Witchcraft (Galatians 5:20)

Drunkenness (Galatians 5:21)

Wild Living (Luke 15:13; Galatians 5:21)

Cheating (1 Corinthians 6:8)

Adultery (1 Corinthians 6:9, 10)

Homosexuality (1 Corinthians 6:9, 10)

Greed (1 Corinthians 6:9, 10 Ephesians 5:5)

Stealing (1 Corinthians 6:9, 10)

Lying (Revelation 22:12-16)

The by-products of living for God are:

Love (Galatians 5:22)

Joy (Galatians 5:22)

Peace (Galatians 5:22)

Patience (Galatians 5:22)

Kindness (Galatians 5:22)

Goodness (Galatians 5:22)

Faithfulness (Galatians 5:22)

Gentleness (Galatians 5:22)

Self-control (Galatians 5:22)

The Story of Job and Wealth

Job Is Tested

Job 1:1-2:13

Job, a wealthy and upright man, lost his possessions, his children, and his health. Job did not understand why he was suffering. Why does God allow his children to suffer? Although there is an explanation, we may not know it while we are here on earth. In the meantime, we must always be ready for testing in our lives.

Three Friends Answer Job

Job 3:1-31:40

Job's friends wrongly assumed that suffering always came as a result of sin. With this in mind, they tried to persuade Job to repent of his sin. The three friends were wrong. Suffering is not always a direct result of personal sin. When we experience severe suffering, it may not be our fault, so we do not have to add to our pain by feeling guilty that some hidden sin is causing our trouble.

A Young Man Answer Job

Job 32:1-37:24

A young man named Elihu, who had been listening to the entire conversation, criticized the three friends for being unable to answer Job. He said that although Job was a good man, he had allowed himself to become proud, and God was punishing him in order to humble him. This answer was partially true because suffering does purify our faith. However, God is beyond our comprehension, and we cannot know why he allows each instance of suffering to come into our lives. Our part is simply to remain faithful.

God Answers Job

Job 38:1-41: 34

God himself finally answered Job. God is in control of the world, and only he understands why the good are allowed to suffer. This only becomes clear to us when we see God for who he is. We must courageously accept what God allows to happen in our lives and remain firmly committed to him.

Job Is Restored

Job 42:1-17

Job finally learned that when nothing else was left, he had God, and that was enough. Through suffering, we learn that God is enough for our lives and our future. WE must love God regardless of whether he allows blessing or sufferings to come to us. Testing is difficult, but the result is often a deeper relationship with God. Those who endure the testing of their faith will experience God's great rewards in the end.

Job 31:24-28 NIV

24 "If I have put my trust in gold
   or said to pure gold, 'You are my security,'
25 if I have rejoiced over my great wealth,
   the fortune my hands had gained,
26 if I have regarded the sun in its radiance
   or the moon moving in splendor,
27 so that my heart was secretly enticed
   and my hand offered them a kiss of homage,
28 then these also would be sins to be judged,
   for I would have been unfaithful to God on high.

Job 31: 24-28 NIV affirmed that depending on wealth for happiness is idolatry and denies the God of heaven. We excuse our society's obsession with money and possessions as a necessary evil or the way it works in the modern world. However, every society in every age has valued the power and prestige that money brings. True believers must purge themselves of the deep-seated desire for more power, prestige, and possessions. They must, also, not withhold their resources from neighbors near and far. who have desperate physical needs.

A Recipe for Success

Ingredients:

a heart

a mind

a soul

1. Grab a book, an article or a short story each day about God's promises; his Word.

2. Read and understand what you are reading. For you, what is the meaning of the words strung into sentences, sentences strung into paragraphs, and paragraphs strung into stories, messages, and so forth? Mix your heart, mind, and soul as you leaf through the pages for thirty minutes.

3. Put a decision in action. What would you like to do with the knowledge you have gained from reading? Use it? Keep it? Share it to others?

If the whole reading experience tastes good, you surely have enjoyed life.

If not, please repeat the first step.

EUREKA BUTLER

Words Have Power

Even though these two encouraging and wisdom filled mothers are not here physical with my family and I, their words still dwell in my heart.

I would like to give a special honor to my mom, Gwendolyn Andrews Smith, for telling me that Manuel was my husband in spite of his then lifestyle. She spoke these words into my life before we were even married. "Manuel is the one that you will marry. You will have some long, rough and hard days. But, hang in there it will be worth it." "Mommy, now I can see what you meant." It is worth it!

My mother-in-law, Elease Williams. "Hume," you just don't know how you cleared my heart of doubts and fears concerning your son and our marriage. I told you I didn't feel as though he "Loves me". Your last encouraging words to me were "Yes he does!" Because when I tried to say something negative about you concerning that car, he put me in my place. You said " I shouldn't have to every worry about his love, because he does!"

To a very special lady that I will never forget. My great grandmother, Elizabeth Andrews, those many days sitting on the front praying over my heart, soul and mind. " I am a Success!"

Auntie Elouise Andrews, for the many rides in the blue car and never complaining about taking my sister and I places; especially the skating rink, " Love you Much!"

Proverbs 4:23 (NIV) "Above all else, guide your heart, for it is the wellspring of life"

Other readings from Eureka Butler:

"HEY" God series:

    Divorce is not an Option

        It's a Stronghold" Published 2013

Connect with Prophetess Eureka Butler at Heyprosperity@gmail.com

Website: HEY-Success.com

Percentage of Books and T-Shirts proceeds will go to the following Food Ministry:

Helping Hands Depot, Inc,

7029 Commonwealth Ave, Suite 10

Jacksonville, Florida 32220

http://helpinghandsdepot.org

<u>SUCCESS</u>

Joshua 1:8 KJV "This book of the law shall not depart out of thy mouth; but thou shalt meditate therein day and night, that thou mayest observe to do according to all that is written therein: for then thou shalt make thy way prosperous and then thou shalt have good success."

References

Holy Bible, New International Version®, NIV® Copyright © 1973, 1978, 1984, 2011 by Biblica, Inc.® Used by permission. All rights reserved worldwide.

Life Application Study Bible, New International Version, Copyright 1988, 1989, 1990, 1991, 2005 by Tindale House Publishers, Inc., Wheaton, IL 608189. All rights reserved.

Scripture taken from the Good News Translation - Second Edition, Copyright 1992 by American Bible Society. Used by Permission.

Scripture quoted by permission. Quotations designated (NIV) are from THE HOLY BIBLE: NEW INTERNATIONAL VERSION®. NIV®. Copyright © 1973, 1978, 1984 by Biblica. All rights reserved worldwide. (New International Version Bible Online)

The Holy Bible, New King James Version Copyright © 1982 by Thomas Nelson, Inc.

The Holy Bible, English Standard Version. Copyright ©2001 by Crossway Bibles, a publishing ministry of Good News Publishers.

The Living Bible copyright © 1971 by Tyndale House Foundation. Used by permission of Tyndale House Publishers Inc., Carol Stream, Illinois 60188. All rights reserved

EUREKA BUTLER

www.ingramcontent.com/pod-product-compliance
Lightning Source LLC
Chambersburg PA
CBHW051706170526
45167CB00002B/561